ROBERT CHAFE

Two Plays

Butler's
Marsh
•
Tempting
Providence

Robert Chafe
Two Plays

Butler's Marsh
Tempting Providence

Playwrights Canada Press
Toronto • Canada

Playwrights Canada Press

215 Spadina Avenue, Suite 230, Toronto, Ontario CANADA M5T 2C7
416-703-0013   fax 416-408-3402
orders@playwrightscanada.com • www.playwrightscanada.com

Financial support provided by the taxpayers of Canada and Ontario through the Canada
Council for the Arts and the Department of Canadian Heritage through the Book
Publishing Industry Development Programme, and the Ontario Arts Council.

The Canada Council for the Arts
Le Conseil des Arts du Canada

ONTARIO ARTS COUNCIL
CONSEIL DES ARTS DE L'ONTARIO

Cover image: Molly Glover on Bragg's Island   © David Blackwood 1997
Etching 32 x 20.
Production Editor: JLArt

National Library of Canada Cataloguing in Publication

Chafe, Robert
    Robert Chafe : two plays : Butler's marsh, Tempting providence.

ISBN 0-88754-722-2

    I. Playwrights Guild of Canada. II. Title. III. Title: Butler's marsh.
IV. Title: Tempting providence.

PS8555.H2655A19 2004   C812'.6   C2004-900079-9

First edition: March 2004. Second printing January 2006.
Printed and bound by AGMV Marquis at Quebec, Canada.

for my parents,
William and Elizabeth Chafe

TABLE OF CONTENTS
— — • — — • — —

— • — Introduction — • —

Newfoundland and Labrador, poor in economic terms, has always been blessed in its artistic wealth. Rich in folklore, steeped in legends, and possessed of a vibrant oral tradition of song and story-telling, the rugged country seems to resonate with the voices and imaginations of its inhabitants. Not surprisingly, writers and artists of every sort have found rich soil here to nourish their roots, and the body of essays, songs, poetry, drama, and visual art that has emerged over the decades has ensured a legacy that will outlast even the pain of a lost fishery, or the temporary joys of off-shore oil.

Robert Chafe is not the most recent of Newfoundland artists; he has been practicing his skills as actor and playwright for more than ten years. Well known to Newfoundland and Labrador audiences, he is an unfamiliar presence outside the province, despite having a number of his plays staged across Canada: like many Newfoundland artists, his career has been a struggle for survival. Working frequently as playwright-to-hire, he has had little opportunity to prepare his own place in the Canadian pantheon. In part, this situation arises because his plays, with the exception of *Charismatic Death Scenes* (*Canadian Theatre Review 98*), have not been published. It is hoped that this edition will be a first step towards rectifying this situation.

Chafe, like most of his compatriots, is a story-teller. His range is wide, from personal myth through fantastic legend to historical past. What defines most clearly his particular talent, however, is the dramatic framework in which such stories are constructed. A new Chafe play is an event of some importance; it is impossible to predict its nature, but it will be new, it will be different, and it will be theatrically exciting.

Chafe has enjoyed the collaboration of two very different directors who in their different ways have fully appreciated his dramatic potential, and done their utmost to realize it on stage. Fellow islanders Jillian Keiley and Danielle Irvine have between them staged the substantial bulk of Chafe's work. Each works in significantly different ways from the other, but both have produced vibrant testimonials to Chafe's abilities as a playwright. Both are distinguished in their own right; Keiley was awarded the John Hirsch Prize for emerging directors in 1998, and Irvine in 2000, but they are very different. As Gordon Jones, St. John's resident theatre critic, writes: "In contrast to Keiley, whose directorial stamp is blazoned on her productions as plainly as a Nike logo, Irvine's effect is more elusive"

(*Performing Arts 31*). For Jones, "Keiley's' shows are characteristically design-driven" while Irvine's "directing is explorative and actor-focused." In reviewing this playwright's production history an almost eerie symmetry is revealed. One production with Irvine is followed by one with Keiley, then back to Irvine and so on. The two plays in this collection follow this pattern with *Butler's Marsh* first produced under Irvine and *Tempting Providence* with Keiley. In examining not only the play texts but their original productions much can be gleamed about Chafe's particular strengths.

Two contrasting pieces, *Under Wraps: A Spoke Opera*, written for Keiley's company Artistic Fraud and discussed in *Canadian Theatre Review 115*, and *Place of First Light* discussed in *Canadian Theatre Review 93*, written for Irvine's company in the same year, 1997, illustrate the point clearly. The Keiley production has two actors performing a tale of unrequited love while a chorus of sixteen performers sing and move beneath a sheet. On the other end of the spectrum is *Place of First Light* produced by Irvine's company. Here is a historical, multi-location pageant about Bell Island's miners, their town and their families. In the former, the strong production elements Jones characterized as Keiley's trademark dominate. In the latter, we have strong actor-driven vignettes, one following after another. Both productions, however, are equally compelling and theatrically exciting.

This contrast continues in 1998 when again Irvine and Keiley take directorial charge of two contrasting Chafe scripts. Irvine directs the playwright-turned-actor in *Charismatic Death Scenes* while Keiley works with Chafe in *Empty Girl*. *Empty Girl* met with mixed results. In fact, while not statistically proven, it would be safe to say that half the audience loved the play and production while the rest either hated the production but liked the play or just plain hated it. In this play, Chafe is exploring the often weird and twisted world of carnival. I was on the hating side, feeling that the production overwhelmed the interesting character-driven script. However, others like reviewer Jones felt otherwise: "Fertile collaboration between designer-director and author-actor converts a naturalistic script into an intricate piece of *son et lumiere* performance theatre expressing the ambiguous interface of truth and depiction in business, show biz, life and love." (*Telegram*, Friday October 1998). *Charismatic Death Scenes* goes in the opposite direction. Where Keiley had a multi-layered approach to her Chafe text, Irvine has the playwright/actor surrounded by four old-fashioned typewriters, a few sheets of paper and an old Christmas present for her total set and props.

The two plays in this collection, *Butler's Marsh* and *Tempting Providence*, both took form in the year 2000, but this is the only similarity that they share. *Butler's Marsh* was workshopped in that year but its roots can probably be traced back to the three years of summer production on Bell Island with Place of First Light Productions. *Tempting Providence* for its part was commissioned by Gros Morne Theatre Festival in 2000. While both plays are clearly, once again, all about story and story-telling, the one is rooted in history while the other is immersed in legend and folk tale. And again, while both can be said to be women's stories, one is clearly a celebration of a life lived and the other is a tale of mystery and intrigue, true or otherwise.

Tempting Providence relates the story of Nurse Myra Bennett's life in Newfoundland, but it is also the history of an outport community and the generation that made that life part of Newfoundland mythology. The nurse's story is a quintessentially Newfoundland saga of isolation and deprivation transformed by the goodness of heart, dedication, and courage found in both individuals and the community. In the process we also learn of life in Daniel's Harbour, glimpse into the world of the coastal nurses and are reminded of the work of the Grenfell Mission. All of which is accomplished extremely simply as Chafe recounts the rich life of British born Myra Bennett. The play begins with her arrival in a small community on Newfoundland's northern peninsula in the 1920s. It is her job to serve this vast roadless community; the lack of a road becomes the beacon that Chafe uses to mark her life of service: "Think you'll have a road in two years? Can't leave you without a nurse. Without a sensible road. It wouldn't be right." While she marries at the end of the first act, at the end of her two-year contract, it is not until the end of the play, following a life of service in Daniel's Harbour, that the road is finally being built. This two-year contract becomes a contract for life, professional and matrimonially, despite all the hardships.

The play is episodic, offering snapshots of a life lived. From her first days in Daniel Harbour, Nurse Bennett, nee Nurse Grimsley, commanded respect:

You will refer to me as Nurse. Nurse. Nurse Grimsley if you prefer, but never miss. And certainly not Mrs. I would demand your respect just as I'm sure you would expect to have mine.

And respect she earns as she serves the vast community, travelling miles by foot when the weather permits and failing that by horse, sledge or boat. We meet the men, women and children of the

Northern Peninsula. We witness childbirth, deaths by breach birth, the fear of TB, teeth being pulled and even an old horse being checked while the young Nurse matures, falls in love with local Angus Bennett, marries and has two children.

Chafe arranges these snapshots in a loosely historical pattern, with Act One closing with the marriage proposal and Act Two quickly moving through childbirth to the near-disastrous event of the accident that happens to her brother-in-law, Alex, when he falls into the saw blade at the mill. Throughout it all, light humourous touches lighten the potentially bleak tale that characterized outport life in the early part of the twentieth century. Nurse Bennett indeed carried a "sadness in her heart," children died at birth, and TB was a real danger. Set against these are the kitchen parties, the communal good-will, and the good done, including a memorable removal of an abscessed tooth on stage. Perhaps the last, and most significant episode best characterizes the multi-layered, multiple perspective that Chafe uses to tell this tale. Word comes down from the logging camp that brother-in-law Alex is injured. His foot was to all intents sheared off. Myra and Angus rush to bring him to their home where she re-attaches the foot, bandages him and they wait for word of the Doctor who is sixty miles away. The Doctor, however, sends back word that they must bring Alex to him. So despite the snow and the lack of road, they pack him in the sled and start off. This journey is not made alone, however:

MYRA
    And. There they are.
ANGUS
    Help.
MYRA
    Eight beautiful souls trekking toward us over the ice.
ANGUS
    Parsons Pond. Must have intercepted our wire.
MYRA
    Intercepted our wire and immediately mobilized to help.
ANGUS
    I was getting afraid for a minute we wouldn't make it.
    The mare.

Every community comes out to help. Husband and wife make the trek and save the foot; what is being celebrated, however, is not only a Nurse's herculean efforts but the neighbouring communities' collective humanity and energy. This is the thrust of *Tempting*

Providence. Nurse Bennett's extraordinary life is celebrated, and it is a celebration that is extended to the entire fabric of outport life at the turn of the century. More particularly, the play is a celebration of the nurses who provided front-line health care in very difficult circumstances, throughout most of Newfoundland for most of its history.

Keiley directed the opening production of *Tempting Providence* for Theatre Newfoundland and Labrador in 2002. Although the play has many different characters, Chafe's cast list includes only Myra, Trevor, and Man and Woman. Actors performing these latter roles shift into and out of different people from Daniel's Harbour. Or as Chafe writes for the Man "various distinct male characters, aged fourteen to eighty." Chafe asks for a bare setting, allowing the play to be almost exclusively actor-driven. In the opening production, four actors performed all the parts dressed in off-white clothes within an open space, using a table, four chairs and a large white tablecloth. Keiley takes a highly stylized approach to the simplicity demanded by Chafe; Jones in his review describes the approach as

"Economically, ingeniously and elegantly, furniture is rearranged and transformed to represent a variety of properties and settings. Table and chairs become beds, doors, sleighs, boats or cribs. The tablecloth serves as cloak, sheet, bread-dough, newborn baby, wedding dress, or tourniquet. (*Telegram*, December 6, 2002)

Keiley's production was indeed extremely effective. At times the Nurse's despair was felt. At others, we laughed with her and applauded her perseverance. Not surprisingly, the production was a hit in Cow Head and also popular when it toured to St. John's. Since then it has been back at Cow Head in Summer 2003 and on the mainland.

In many ways, *Butler's Marsh* is a study in contrasts to *Tempting Providence.* Here is a two character play set in Bell Island, a tiny island off the Avalon Peninsula in eastern Newfoundland, in the present. Its source is legend or myth rather than history and while it too has a female protagonist, there is nothing of Nurse Bennett in Nora. Finally, opening at the LSPU Hall in St. John's on September 19, 2001, a time in which the entire island was playing host to plane-fulls of reluctant tourists who had been forbidden entry to American air space after the events of September 11, it played to small audiences. However, *Butler's Marsh*, like *Tempting Providence*, is again finally about stories and story-telling, and again Chafe with competence and assurance pulls in his audience.

The characters in the play are a young woman named Nora and a young man, Tim. Nora's mother was originally from Bell Island but Nora was born in Ontario. Nora and Tim have travelled back to the island, because Nora apparently wants to discover truths about her mother's past. As the play progresses, any sense of certainty the audience might have concerning the significance of the events of the play is undermined, until the dramatic ending leaves the audience reassessing all that has proceeded. Like *Tempting Providence, Butler's Marsh* is very simply imagined. Another character-driven piece, this play demands a simple playing space and two actors. Chafe relies on simple lighting to highlight and support the structure of the play.

The play begins with Nora alone in darkness, apparently searching for a flashlight. When she discovers it, we see her kneeling by the knapsack, using it to briefly illuminate her surroundings. As she does, one of the central themes of the play emerges in her thoughts: "And as long as I can see the stars I'm not lost. I am not lost. I am not lost." Immediately following this speech is a huge flash of light and Tim appears asking her if she is lost. Trying to find something and being lost or not being lost are common threads in *Butler's Marsh* as Tim and Nora appear to be trying to clarify past events.

Nora has returned to Bell Island to discover why her mother came to this marsh. This area in Bell Island resonates with many stories like those told to Nora by a man at the local garage. He claims there are "little people"; Tim calls them pixies. He obviously does not believe the tales, but Nora counters with a story that occurred twenty years before her mother went missing in the marsh for three days. Again, Tim doesn't believe it and so they go back and forth while Chafe textures their world with increased darkness and sounds of the wind. A sense of unease at the beginning is heightened as Chafe plays with the surroundings. First the wind is there and then it is not. The flash of light at the beginning is balanced by the flash near the end. A horrible smell marks the moments before the climax and the trees begin to shake. The mystery and fear permeates the theatre. The play ends with Nora alone again.

The first production of *Butler's Marsh* was directed by Danielle Irvine for the Resource Centre for the Arts Theatre. Irvine chose to emphasize the eerie world that Chafe's script creates by staging the play in the round. Using a circle of tree stumps on which audience members were encouraged to sit, she centered the action in a tight central area on the LSPU performing space.

The production was all about performance, and it was this aspect in particular that drew critical praise from Jones: "Two actors with contrasting voices but complementary on-stage presence, Tilley and Winters, made the most of a cleverly crafted script and an effective production design" (*Telegram*, September 21, 2001). Audiences too were enthusiastic, though unhappily small as a result of the turmoil in the city after the terrorist attacks of 9/11.

Tempting Providence and *Butler's Marsh* represent only two examples of Chafe's expanding body of dramatic work, which includes ten plays completed to date with one currently under way for Theatre Newfoundland Labrador and Stephenville Festival. He was made Playwright-in-Residence for Artistic Fraud in 2003 and is presently collaborating on two more pieces for this company. He also continues to work as an actor, most recently creating finely-crafted character pieces in *Salvage: A Story of a House*. In a limited way, these plays published here are Newfoundland stories. Chafe's Nurse Bennett clearly stems from a particular point in this island's past just as the legend of Bell Island originally resonates from that tiny island. However in crafting these pieces, Chafe is able, as usual, to move beyond the immediate and capture more fundamental human portraits that speak past provincial boundaries. This publication will, of course, introduce readers to Chafe's work but it is hoped that it will also introduce playgoers to the mysteries of Nora and the fortitude of Myra. Finally, this publication, it can be hoped, will lead to the publication of more of this playwright's fine work.

—Denyse Lynde
St. John's, Newfoundland

Denyse Lynde is a Professor at Memorial University of Newfoundland and Labrador where she teaches in theatre and media. Her research interests lie in the theatre and drama of Newfoundland and she has published in *Canadian Theatre Review* and *Theatre Research in Canada*. She was editor for *Voices from the Landwash* (Playwrights Canada Press).

Butler's Marsh

A mere forty-minute voyage from Newfoundland's capital city St. John's, Bell Island sits in the middle of Conception Bay, a towering fortress of one-hundred-foot cliffs and blood-red iron rich soil. By day the view from its dizzying edge is an array of sea, air, and the dramatic rocky face of the mainland coast. By night it is surrounded by the blackness of the unlit North Atlantic, and the twinkling bowl of lights betraying communities nestled around the bay. It is an artist's dream, with its physical beauty matched only by the wealth of stories that have walked its shores and tunnelled its earth.

Butler's Marsh is a small patch of wet woodland located in the heart of the most populated area of Bell Island. Pretty much every Bell Islander, at least one point in their lives, was told to stay out of Butler's Marsh. People tell stories of the now near famous fairies of Newfoundland. There is as much history here as there would be in any book about Cabot, the Vikings, and Confederation combined. It is a social phenomena hailing from our deep Irish and English roots. Legends and "true" tales of people vanishing for days, even weeks at a time, only to return home safely but looking like they had wrestled a bear. Fragmented accounts would emerge that spoke of the little people, who were often kind, and more often not. People were warned to carry crusts of bread as peace offerings, or to learn to speak their name or the Lord's prayer backwards for immediate counteractive magic to the fairies' trap. Parents told their children to avoid certain areas in the community, often wooded and empty. Many of these areas offer rational basis to extrapolate real reason for these warnings. A dangerous cliff. Forest big enough to get lost in. Some do not. Some are small and benign and impossibly close. Like Butler's Marsh. For these places, the stories still thrive even if the factual basis for their evolution is still well open for speculation. This is a play about myth, stories, and fact behind fiction.

Butler's Marsh was originally workshopped through Playwright's Atlantic Resource Centre's Moveable Feast, Playwright's Colony in Victoria by the Sea, PEI, September 2000, with dramaturgy by Don Hannah.

The play was further developed by *Lunchbox Theatre's Stage One Play Development Program* in Calgary Alberta, May 2001, with dramaturgy by Johanne Deleeuw.

It was premiered by *Resource Centre for the Arts Theatre* in St. John's Newfoundland on September 20, 2001 with the following company:

NORA Sara Tilley
TIM   Phil Winters

Directed by Danielle Irvine
Stage Managed by Diana Haynes
Assistant Stage Managed by Kim Brothers
Set Design by Michael Slack
Lighting Design by Diana Haynes
Costume Design by Barry Buckle
Production Management by Ann Brophy

— • — — • — — • —

This play was written with generous assistance from the Canada Council for the Arts and the Newfoundland and Labrador Arts Council. Its existence owes much to Danielle Irvine, Anna Stassis, First Light Productions (cast and crew), and the fine people of Bell Island, most notably Henry and Kay Crane.

—•— Characters —•—

Nora A woman in her late twenties. Urban and stylish, she should look out of place and unprepared.

Tim A controlled and confident man in his early thirties. He has a rumbling intensity which is at turns wildly erotic and then indefinably unsettling.

—•— Setting —•—

A small clearing in the densely forested Butler's Marsh. Walls of living gnarled trees, and, beyond their branches, darkness. Forest floor is solid, but damp. Sky above black, with traces of stars. Despite the tiniest hint of man-made light in the sky from a nearby settlement, there is an overwhelming feeling of seclusion. This could be either prison or hideaway.

BUTLER'S MARSH

Perfect darkness that goes on a little too long. A noise. A twig breaking. Breathing. Someone is moving through trees. Breathing is restless. Staggered. There is another noise from elsewhere. The breathing stops. Waiting. Silence. A voice.

NORA
Hello?

Long pause. Complete silence.

Nothing.

She is moving awkwardly in the darkness. A loud crack and a grunt of frustration. And then calm breathing to recover.

A light. A light a light a light a light.

A flashlight breaks the dark.

A light.

She kneels in a huddle next to a knapsack and its contents which she had removed in her search for the light. She scans the flashlight over the surrounding trees.

Hello?

Complete silence. She reaches into the bag once more and removes a dark blanket. She quietly begins to unwrap it and lay it on the ground. Once in place she slowly and gently fixes one of its corners. She begins to replace the items in her backpack. She pauses when she finds a small photo. She lays it softly on the blanket and gazes at it.

Look at you. What would you have me do? What would you have me tell them?

She hears something. Water trickling.

A river. No. No one mentioned a river.

She puts the photo in her pocket and stands to look for the river.

Why didn't he mention a river? It's important. He should have told me about a river.

She finds it. Her flashlight beam dances on its surface and reflects to her face, illuminating her for the first time.

A river. No path. No... moon. But, I can still see the sky. I can
still see the sky. And the stars. And as long as I can see the stars
I'm not lost. I am not lost. I am not lost.

There is a brilliant flash of light that engulfs the entire space.
NORA is startled and her eyes hurt from the glow.

Goddamn it. God. What the hell was that? God.

She blinks hard to recover.

TIM
You're not lost?

NORA
Tim?

TIM emerges easily from the woods. He is smiling.

TIM
Yes.

NORA
You frightened me.

TIM
Are you sure you're not lost?

NORA
Don't do that. Creep up like that.

He loses his smile.

TIM
Sorry.

NORA
You really frightened me Tim. You did. There was no light,
I couldn't see a thing and you weren't around and then there
was this... this.... Did you see that?

TIM
What?

NORA
There was this, this huge flash. Or something.

TIM
Really.

NORA
It. Yeah, Tim. You didn't see that?

TIM
Are you okay?

NORA
You're kidding me right?

TIM
I just want to know if you are okay.

NORA
Yeah. I was. Just... don't do that. Again.

TIM
Sorry. I won't. Are you tired?

NORA
No. Not yet.

TIM
Are you getting sick?

NORA
What?

TIM
Are you feeling sick?

NORA
In the head?

A pause as she looks at him for a reaction.

I did see something, Tim.

TIM
I believe you.

There is a slight pause.

NORA
You're smiling.

TIM
Yes?

NORA
Don't. It's... inappropriate. To say you believe me and then smile like that.

TIM
Okay. I'll remember that. I'll try to remember as best I can.

There is a tense pause.

NORA
Here.

> *She tosses him the light, and begins to dig in her bag again. He points the light at her, but then notices the blanket and lights it.*

TIM
What are you doing?

NORA
I've got another.

TIM
What?

NORA
Another light. Can you help me out here. Some light?

TIM
I meant here. What are you doing, here.

NORA
Closer, Tim.

TIM
Yes.

NORA
Closer.

TIM
Yes?

NORA
Tim?

> *She stands and turns. He is very close.*

TIM
Closer?

NORA
No. I got it.

> *She grabs his light again and returns to the bag.*

TIM
I'm sorry.

NORA
Pretty tasteless.

TIM
What's that?

NORA
Your... advances. Now. After everything.

TIM
You're angry.

She stands again and points her light at him. A brief pause.

NORA
Where were you? Just now.

TIM
Not quite sure. I was exploring. It's pretty thick in there.

NORA
I thought you were here. With me. All the time.

TIM
Were you afraid?

NORA
That's not the point. We just shouldn't get separated. There's no moon now, no light. It's too dark.

She tosses him the spare light she found.

Confusing.

TIM
Safest place in the world

NORA
Well at least tell me, anything interesting? In there.

TIM
Trees. Grass. Dark.

He turns his light on.

NORA
Anything else?

TIM
Are you looking for something specific?

NORA
I think that's fairly obvious.

TIM
What exactly?

NORA
We'll know when we find it.

TIM
Well, I didn't find it. Back there.

NORA
It's cold. You cold?

TIM
Never.

NORA
God, the air is so crisp. It's beautiful here.

TIM
Yes. It is.

A small pause as she looks at him.

NORA
You think so?

TIM
Yeah.

She releases a small smile.

What.

NORA
Nothing. That's just, surprising. You never had a kind word to say. About Newfoundland.

TIM
Well, I'm here.

NORA
You never had any interest in coming here until I asked you not to. I wanted to do this alone but you insisted–

TIM
I can't let you wander here alone.

A small pause. She turns away from him and lights the surrounding trees.

NORA
Safest place in the world, right? Good place for her to be. To be lost. As good a place as any. It could have been worse.

TIM
Yeah?

NORA
Could have been darker. Even darker. And even colder. Could have been winter. She could have died.

TIM
Yes. She could have.

NORA
You never did tell me your theories.

TIM
Why she didn't freeze to death?

NORA
Why she was here in the first place.

TIM
My theories aren't important.

NORA
But I know you have them. And I know you'll tell me. Speak them aloud. Unlike just about everyone else.

TIM
It is beautiful here.

NORA
And?

TIM
And, she didn't freeze to death. She made it out of here alive. That's important.

NORA
God. You sound like Aunt Shirley. Only telling me, repeating to me how they found her, what she was like. That she made it out of here alive. That's what was important. I don't need that Tim. I have heard nothing but rumour and innuendo. I don't need reassurance or comforting.

TIM
You are so angry at me.

His frankness abates her.

NORA
No one will tell me anything, Tim. About Mom, this place. Even this island. Nothing useful. Or satisfying. She was in here for three days. Three days and three nights.

TIM
There are three days worth of beauty here.

NORA
I think there are major holes in your hypothesis sir.

He gives her a shy smile.

TIM
Shall we test it?

There is a slight pause. She smiles at him.

NORA
You... jerk. Part of me, part of me actually likes this. You being here. I hate that.

TIM
You wouldn't prefer to be alone?

NORA
Thought I would. But now that we are here. No. No, I don't want to be alone.

TIM
Good.

NORA
I'm. Sorry. I'm sorry I told you not to come.

TIM
I know.

NORA
Do you blame me? After what you said. After what you said to me at the airport.

TIM
You want to talk about it?

NORA
No. No I don't. Not as long as you're here. And you're okay.

TIM
I am. You?

NORA
Yeah. Fine. A little hungry. Do you have any food?

TIM
You sure you don't want to talk about it?

NORA
No. Never again if you please, just... just tell me that you have some of those lovely little cakes you've made me so fond of.

TIM
Sorry.

NORA
Left everything in the car?

TIM
Yes.

> *She begins to rummage in her backpack.*

NORA
Well, we will have to make do with... cigarettes... and breath mints.

TIM
Since you're not lost, and since you are so fond of those lovely little cakes, why don't you run back to the car.

NORA
I'm not lost.

TIM
Then go.

NORA
I'm not that hungry.

TIM
You will want those cakes later.

> *She speaks a little too loudly.*

NORA
Then I will go later.

> *A small pause.*

TIM
Okay.

NORA

I'm not lost, Tim. Everything is exactly how it was described to me.

TIM

Dark?

NORA

Except. Do you remember them saying there was a river here? Do you remember that guy at the gas station saying that?

TIM

I wasn't listening.

NORA

I'm sure he said that the ground was wet in places. Marshy. He must have... neglected to...

TIM

Reliable source for sure.

NORA

But everything else, everything is as he described it.

TIM

Maybe you are being misled.

NORA

How ironic. Me, being lied to.

A short pause.

That was meant to be funny.

TIM

Okay.

NORA

I. I don't think I was being lied to. Tim. I assure you he was harmless. A little excitable perhaps, but ultimately harmless.

TIM

Were you exciting the locals? You can't be left alone.

NORA

He needed no help from me.

TIM

And it was by the words of this man, this excitable man, that we find ourselves on the banks of this surprising river.

NORA

He was the only one who would even talk to me about this place.

TIM

What?

NORA

Most people here. I walk up and ask them, mention her name, or mention this place, and they just, just look at me like I'm speaking another language.

TIM

But he talked to you.

NORA

It's just strange. This river. He did know lots about what was in here.

TIM

You don't sound confident in that.

NORA

Tim.

TIM

What? You don't. You look confused. Tired.

NORA

I'm not tired.

TIM

Shaken. Afraid of the dark.

NORA

I'm not... I'm not afraid.

TIM

He has shaken you.

NORA

I'm not talking about this with you. I'm sure you would just find it...

TIM

What?

NORA

Humourous.

TIM

What did he say to you?

NORA
Just.

TIM
Just?

NORA
Stories.

He smiles at her.

Unbelievable stories.

TIM
Do tell.

NORA
Not sure I can. Not while I'm in here.

TIM
He scared you. You're scared.

NORA
Not yet. No. No I'm not.

TIM
You should go.

NORA
No.

TIM
You really should go.

NORA
I'm not leaving. Not yet.

TIM
Well. He was wrong about the river, I'm sure he was wrong about the ghosts.

NORA
He wasn't talking about ghosts. And he wasn't wrong about everything. He knows this place. He even mentioned that, that little love-heart etched in the tree back there. Size, shape.

TIM
Maybe he carved it.

NORA
You should have been listening.

TIM
What?

NORA
You should have been listening to him. You wanted to come here. This is important.

TIM
Yes. I believe it is.

NORA
Tim. Really. You should have been there. You should have been listening.

TIM
Sorry. Guess I was...

NORA
What?

TIM
Lost. In the stars.

He looks at her and smiles. She softens and smiles.

NORA
See. You're being led. They gotcha now.

TIM
Pardon me?

NORA
Gotcha all enchanted with the stars. Old trick.

TIM
Really.

NORA
Apparently.

TIM
You're going to scare yourself.

NORA
Lucky you're here to save me.

TIM
Yes.

NORA
It is beautiful here. Smaller than I thought it would be. Not Bell Island really, just this place. Barely big enough to be a sensible backyard. But, it is beautiful.

TIM
I've said so.

NORA
I bet in the day, during the day you can see the Green from here. That's that section of town. Just to the north. This way. No, this way.

TIM
That's north.

NORA
Yeah? Can't be far. I'm surprised you can't see the lights. Mom and Dad rented a house over there. The year before they were married, just before they moved to Cambridge. Way before me, or they even thought about kids but, but they couldn't live with Grandpa anymore. He wouldn't have it, not before the wedding.

He is staring at her smiling.

You're smiling.

TIM
Sorry.

NORA
No. Like you remember. Like it's your history. It's nice. It's, I don't know... inclusive.

TIM
It's this place. There is something.

NORA
It's winning you over. Clean air.

TIM
Yes.

NORA
No traffic. No sirens. No sound at all. Just the wind.

TIM
Magic.

NORA
Yeah. Let's buy it.

TIM

What?

NORA

Let's buy it. Some of this land.

TIM

This land?

NORA

Yeah. It would be nice. To have some of it in the family again. Some of the island.

TIM

You want to buy this land?

NORA

Sure. I mean I'm sure it's cheap. Undeveloped. And we could... I don't know... because who knows where we will be in a few years, right.

TIM

You don't even know if it is for sale.

NORA

We could ask. In town.

TIM

You assume that it would be for sale. That it could be for sale.

NORA

Tim. I'm just saying that it could be an investment.

TIM

Sure. You're right. I'm sorry you're right. Let's buy it. This land. Bell Island. The whole place.

NORA

Tim.

TIM

Gotta be cheap. Let's buy it all. You could build a bungalow. A little yellow bungalow with hedges and flowers and concrete garden gnomes.

NORA

You're making fun of me.

TIM

No really. You could buy up a huge chunk of it and plow it all
down. Burn it to the ground and erect your perfect dream home.
A place to retire.

NORA

I just thought it would be nice.

TIM

There is potential here. I mean look around. That's all this place
is right? Potential.

NORA

I think it's more than that.

TIM

Is it?

NORA

Yes. It–

TIM

I don't see it. I have to be honest. I don't. Pretty trees. Sure. But
this island's got enough pretty trees. Could stand to lose a few.

NORA

I thought it was winning you over.

TIM

A little dream home. Yeah. I mean this place can't belong to
anybody. You could spend quiet summers here. Retreat to
civilization when the days get shorter and the wind picks up.

NORA

Tim.

TIM

I mean the house will always be here. Useless and empty and
waiting.

NORA

No, Tim, seriously look me in the eye and tell me. Say, Nora,
I would rather live in an apartment building, in the middle of an
urban sprawl.

TIM

I know my place. Nora.

A small pause.

NORA
Well. Good for you.

TIM
Nora.

NORA
It's amazing to me, Tim. I see this fire, this spark behind your eyes and I think I recognize it as, as something else and then it burns me. Without a second thought. Like a stranger.

TIM is staring at her. There is a small pause.

I just thought it would be nice to spend some time here. To have the option.

TIM
Three days of beauty, Nora. I challenge you. Three days. Spend three days in this place and tell me you belong here. Tell me there is room for you here.

NORA
You know what, it won't even take three days.

TIM
Just one night?

NORA
I won't have to keep you here for three days. I feel closer already. I know there is something here.

TIM
Waiting for you in the dark?

NORA
Justification. Rational explanations.

TIM
Have you ever thought, considered that maybe this explanation you're looking for is something that you shouldn't be looking for. Fodder for a lifetime of sleepless nights. Nightmares. Ugly stuff.

NORA
Very dramatic, Tim.

TIM
You wanted to hear my theories.

NORA
Well, I've heard this one before. On the playground. Bathroom walls.

TIM
From kids.

NORA
Dad called it all filth. Said the only thing more nosy and talkative than a bunch of Newfoundlanders was a bunch of Newfoundlanders exiled to Ontario. Said they didn't have the shitty weather to complain about in Cambridge so they had to exercise their tongues somehow. What's your excuse?

TIM
Think about it. It could be ugly.

NORA begins to make fun of his seriousness, but it is infectious.

NORA
Kidnapped? Enchanted by the stars? Led and taken hostage?

TIM
I don't know. Worse. Maybe worse.

NORA
Worse? Like... what. Like?

TIM
Like...

NORA
What? Assaulted?

TIM
Maybe.

There is a slight pause.

NORA
Maybe.

TIM
She was out here for three days.

NORA
Yes. She was.

TIM
So there's an explanation. What do you think of that?

NORA
It's. Extreme.

TIM
So is living in the woods for three days.

NORA

Are you trying to upset me?

TIM

The thought had to have crossed your mind.

NORA

Yes. But there are other possibilities, other explanations that... that are less ugly. That deserve... attention.

TIM

You're right. She was camping.

NORA

I don't think that's very funny.

TIM

It's a less extreme possibility.

NORA

You know how she was found Tim. You know the condition she was in. You know that this wasn't... a... camping trip.

TIM

Just offering options.

NORA

She was out here for three days. They found her comatose. No coat no blanket. Blood on her face. They got her back in town and saw all this blood. She was covered in blood Tim.

TIM

Sounds ugly to me.

NORA

I know how it sounds.

TIM

What are you looking for out here? Tonight.

NORA

I told you–

TIM

Justification? I don't think you want it. I don't.

NORA

God. She was my mother Tim. Attempt, please attempt, to show a little compassion. Regardless of how uncharacteristic.

TIM
> Why are you here?

NORA
> I've told you.

TIM
> The hunt for rational explanations, but nothing too ugly.

NORA
> Tim–

TIM
> Why are you here? Really. Now.

NORA
> July?

TIM
> Night. At night.

NORA
> I...

TIM
> Surely there would be more to see tomorrow. But you chose to be here at night.

NORA
> Don't, don't ask questions like that.

TIM
> Like what?

NORA
> Questions that imply. Questions that accuse.

TIM
> Imply what?

NORA
> Tim–

TIM
> What was I implying?

NORA
> Leave it.

TIM
> Nora.

NORA

Leave it, I said.

TIM

No.

There is a very brief pause. She looks around her.

Nora.

NORA

Did you feel that?

TIM

Why are you here tonight? I want to know.

NORA

The wind. Just stopped.

TIM

Don't change the subject.

NORA

Did you feel that?

TIM

Nora.

NORA

Everything just stopped moving. The trees.

TIM

They're waiting for your answer.

She looks at him. A short pause.

NORA

Why do you ask questions like that? Two days ago you were spitting insults at me. You couldn't give a shit.

TIM

Answer me.

NORA

You don't care.

TIM

I'm standing in the middle of the woods with you. If you don't believe that I care you can at least appreciate the need for conversation.

There is a pause.

Nora?

NORA
Jesus, Tim. You don't...

TIM
Yes? Yes?

NORA
You don't know. This is not some idea that just occurred to me, yesterday. There is a history here.

TIM
Of course.

NORA
Since I was a kid, a little kid, I was always the girl with the crazy mother who flipped out in the woods. You don't know what that's like. Hearing family secrets on the playground. Being told in school that you were probably adopted and being told by your family absolutely nothing.

TIM
You didn't answer the question.

NORA
I don't know. I don't know what I'm looking for here.

TIM
Why tonight?

NORA
Because, because I've waited long enough. I've asked too many questions and gotten nothing.

TIM
You should ask the right people.

NORA
You think I wouldn't ask Mom, now. Or Dad. If they were here. You think I wouldn't demand an answer. I wish I had the wherewithal when she was diagnosed, got sick. But she died, Tim. And Dad not long after. I was ten years old and I lost both of my parents and I was little preoccupied. I was a little too preoccupied to go wading through the questions they left.

TIM
They could have left you with something worse.

NORA
Such as?

TIM
Answers.

NORA
Answers would have been welcome, I assure you.

TIM
Well, welcome them. All of them.

NORA
What?

TIM
Somebody has been talking to you. Telling you stories. There could be answers there.

NORA
What, the gas station guy?

TIM
You said he was the only person here that would talk to you about this place.

NORA
No answers. Just stories. No doubt meant to scare me out of my intentions and into a room in his Bed and Breakfast.

TIM
Scary stories.

NORA
I hate to admit.

TIM
But you said they were unbelievable.

NORA
They are. They are unbelievable. And I don't believe them. At all. It's just.

TIM
Frightening.

NORA
Silly... really.

TIM
I'm listening.

NORA
They have stories about these.... They call them the Little
People.

> *TIM pauses a moment. He smiles.*

TIM
What, like dwarves?

NORA
No.

TIM
Bands of savage dwarves roaming through the woods.

> *NORA herself is now smiling and attempting not to laugh.*

NORA
It was scary, scarier than that. They were mean.

TIM
Mean dwarves.

NORA
Some of these stories. I'm serious.

TIM
The Little People.

NORA
Or the Good People.

TIM
They sound ferocious.

NORA
They did. They did sound ferocious. You should have heard this
guy.

> *She is more serious now.*

TIM
Fairies or something?

NORA
You're not supposed to call them that.

TIM
What?

NORA
You're not supposed to call them that.

TIM
> It offends them?

> *NORA gives a weak little nod.*

And you don't believe this stuff?

NORA
> No.

TIM
> Really.

NORA
> I don't. But...

TIM
> Little people.

NORA
> Do you think that there are things beyond our range, our range of comprehension? Don't you think there's stuff out there like that.

TIM
> Fairies?

NORA
> Stuff that we don't know about, not meant to know about.

TIM
> Do you? Do you think there is stuff like that?

NORA
> I. I don't know. I mean I'm not pompous enough to believe that twenty-first century man has got it all figured out.

TIM
> What about twenty-first century woman?

NORA
> Me?

> *TIM nods. NORA thinks about this and starts up again.*

There is a big part of me that entertains the idea. I do. To a point.

TIM
> But when people start talking about little people with paper wings?

NORA

He wasn't talking about Tinkerbelle.

TIM

Little people in the woods that... that what? Bite your ankles? Fly bites?

NORA

Twenty years before Mom, a ten-year-old boy went missing here. Apparently he came in to look for a small herd of sheep that had gotten away from his father's fold. He didn't come home for supper. He didn't come home for breakfast. They eventually found him in here. He was... curled up around the base of a tree. Naked. Crying. He was covered in blood. His head. Everywhere. But. It wasn't his own. He had found his sheep. They were ripped open and scattered. But not eaten. They brought him to the doctor. He was uncontrollable. Stammering and crying. No words just.... Physically he was fine except for a cut on his leg which was stuffed with twigs and rags and gull bones. And clumps of his own hair. Which had been.... That happened here.

TIM

Did it?

He looks at her. There is a pause.

Did it occur to you that maybe this guy, this gas station guy, was having a good laugh at frightening you. Giving you a good scare before you went off to spend the night alone in the woods?

NORA

No.

TIM

That didn't occur to you?

NORA

It's not possible.

TIM

It's not.... Why isn't that possible?

NORA

Because I met him. The little boy.

TIM

What?

NORA

I met him.

TIM
You met him?

NORA
I was introduced to him. He's sixty. He's sixty now and he's... incomprehensible. He's... barely able to walk. They even showed me his scar.

TIM
And he told you this happened to him?

NORA
He didn't really tell me anything. The guy... the gas station guy told me.

TIM
He could still be playing with you. Using this sad little man as a visual aid, as it were. I mean this invalid might not even speak English, you know.

NORA
He knew. He knew what we were talking about.

TIM
How do you know that?

NORA
Because... he said so.

TIM
What?

NORA
He, he has a two word vocabulary. Two word answer. To every question.

TIM
Two words?

She nods.

Which are?

NORA does not respond.

Which are?

She speaks very softly.

NORA
Butler's Marsh.

There is a lengthy pause.

TIM

Are you actually considering the possibility that your Mother was captured by Pixies?

NORA

I didn't say that.

TIM

Is this the kind of rational explanation you are looking for?

NORA

It's not supposed to be an explanation. It's just creepy is all. This guy was talking about how they catch you, enchant you. Fence you in. Punish trespassers. How time slips and hours become days and days become weeks. She was here for three days Tim. She was covered in blood.

TIM

Sounds like you're formulating an explanation.

NORA

Everyone else I talked to, that I asked, wouldn't tell me anything, Tim. It was like they were terrified of this place. People who live a stones throw from here, but who have never dared to come in. Adults. Don't you think that's strange?

TIM

Stories, Nora. Told to them when they were kids. Stories. Every town has them.

NORA

I know but... most towns have a reason, you know. A dangerous cliff, forest big enough to get lost in. A reason, a practical reason behind the stories to scare kids away from what could hurt them. But this place. I mean look at this place. People come out of this place with these horrible horrible stories. But, no practical reason.

TIM

But, there is a practical reason.

She looks at him.

Whatever happened to your mother.

A small pause.

NORA

It's creepy. The coincidence. It's, it's just a story. I know that. I was just relaying it. It wasn't meant to be an explanation. If anything, it's an explanation as to why I'm shaking like a leaf even though it's the middle of July and I'm wearing a winter coat.

TIM

It's a cold night. Too cold to be out.

NORA

I'm not leaving.

TIM

She survived, Nora. She survived this.

A small pause.

NORA

I know.

TIM

So you better be sure of what you are looking for. You better be sure that rational explanations are really what you want.

NORA

What else would I be looking for?

TIM

Peace.

NORA

Same thing.

TIM

Doesn't have to be.

NORA

Why are you saying this?

TIM

Because, you want to survive this. Don't you?

She stares at him. There is a slight pause. She breaks the stare.

NORA

I don't want to consider that anymore.

TIM

Consider what?

NORA
Leaving empty handed. I don't.

TIM
Well then, we could be here for a while. You must know that.

NORA
Tim.

TIM
It's just important to me, that you know that. If I'm going to stay here. Support you in this.

NORA
You want to support me?

TIM
Yes.

NORA
Well know this. I'm here, tonight, for answers. I'm leaving here with answers. Facts. Regardless of what they might be. And. I'm not leaving otherwise. I'm not.

There is a pause as they stare at each other.

The wind.

TIM
What?

NORA
Just came back. Feel that?

TIM
Didn't notice.

NORA
Dancing in the trees there.

TIM
We should go.

NORA
What? No.

TIM
The wind picks up it's only going to get colder.

NORA
I'll live.

TIM

We can't see anything out here tonight, anyway. Stumbling around in the dark.

NORA

But this is why we came.

TIM

To freeze to death. No, let's go.

NORA

Tim, this is important to me.

TIM

Nora...

NORA

Please. Tim. I'm not leaving. I'm not.

A short pause.

TIM

I am offering you a hand, a helping hand here. Regardless of your ambitions, regardless of your expectations, you should seriously consider your next move. You should seriously take pause to decide what you want from me.

NORA

Just... patience, Tim. It's all, all I need.

TIM

Nora.

NORA

And, I know, I've asked before. I know, I've asked for patience before and you've given it, you've been good, you have even when I.... I didn't want you to come Tim, I didn't, but you came with me anyway and, and now that you're here, I, want you to stay. I can't make you, but I do want you to, Tim. Please. It's important.

He walks away from her. A pause.

Tim?

TIM

Okay. Just remember this.

NORA

Thanks.

TIM
And don't thank me.

NORA
Tim? I. I want you to know that this will be worth it. This will all be worth it. It's gonna make it better. Us better. Being here. I want to tell you that. I just don't want you to, resent. Staying.

TIM
Don't worry about me.

NORA
But I do.

TIM
Don't. I'll entertain myself.

NORA
This will be worth it, Tim. It will. No more questions after tonight. You hear me? No more mysteries in here.

Pause.

You cold?

TIM
No.

NORA
I'm cold. Tim? There's a thick blanket in the car.

TIM
Is there?

NORA
I'm going to get it. You want to come?

TIM
You're just going to come right back.

NORA
Come on. It's just a minute. Change of scenery.

TIM
I can change my scenery whenever I want, Nora. Remember that.

NORA
Tim.

TIM
Which way?

NORA
Don't be like this.

TIM
Which way?

> *A pause as she looks at him. She points her light.*

NORA
That way.

TIM
You sure?

NORA
Yes. It's that way. I walked in through those two trees and saw the river.

TIM
It's pretty thick in here.

NORA
It's the right way. I came in and saw that engraved tree and kept walking.

TIM
Which tree?

NORA
This one with the... heart.

> *Pause.*

TIM
Are you sure?

NORA
Yeah. It was... it was this one.

TIM
There's nothing there.

NORA
No. Maybe it was the other one. Over there.

TIM
Here?

> *NORA nods. TIM shakes his head.*

NORA
So. What? We're lost?

TIM
Which way is the car?

NORA
Fifty feet past the heart.

TIM
That's great, but there is no heart.

NORA
I saw it, Tim.

TIM
You saw it.

NORA
What.

TIM
Nothing.

NORA
Don't look at me that way. I hate it when you look at me that way.

TIM
Nora, which way is the car?

NORA
Don't look at me that way!

TIM
Which way is the car?

NORA
I am not lying, Tim.

> *A small pause.*

TIM
You either know where the car is. Or. You don't.

NORA
I just told you I was cold, and I wanted to go to the car to....
Why would I tell you that if...

TIM
I don't know.

NORA
Tim.

TIM
> What.

NORA
> Tim. This... can't be like this.

> *There is a pause. They stare at each other.*

> You can't... you can't come here and... and hold a grudge.

TIM
> I'm not.

NORA
> You think I'm lying to you again.

> *Pause. TIM stares at her.*

> Tim, you think that, and that mistrust, that ugly look is the reason I was fully prepared to come here alone.

> *Pause. TIM stares at her.*

> If this is what it's still going to be, I could, we could have used this time apart.

> *Pause. TIM stares at her.*

> So.

TIM
> So. Tell me.

NORA
> Tell you what?

TIM
> Tell me.

NORA
> I... I've told you.

TIM
> Tell me.

NORA
> I've told you. I said I was sorry.

TIM
> Tell me.

NORA

Tim. You have to trust me again. I was afraid. Your opinion was very strong and never hidden.

TIM

Tell me where the car is.

NORA

Tim.

TIM

I just want to know where the car is.

NORA

I don't know! I don't know where the car is.

A small pause.

TIM

Well. We are officially lost.

NORA

This place is the size of a backyard. There are houses all around us. We can't be lost. Tim?

TIM

Can't see the stars anymore. Bank of fog ate the entire island. No north star anymore.

NORA

I'm cold. Tim?

She moves to hug him. He backs away speaking directly to her.

TIM

No car. No engraved heart.

He turns his back on her.

NORA

You know what your problem is?

TIM

Only gonna get colder. We should start a fire.

NORA

You never asked the right questions. Or any questions.

TIM

Maybe we can burn our way out.

NORA

You never asked what it meant, what it would mean for me.

TIM

Gonna have to torch the place for the dream home anyway.

NORA

I felt a profound sense of... absence.

TIM looks at her. There is a pause.

You never asked about what I was feeling. You never considered that there were consequences. For me. A reason, to not tell you. To... lie to you.

TIM

Consequences?

NORA

Absence. I felt like I had done something horribly wrong. Like there was an entire world of possibilities that I had erased. Our best laid plans were going to hell and mixed up with the fear and disbelief and surprise of it all I was feeling this weird knot of loss and, and a complete lack of freedom. A complete lack of freedom and that scared me more than anything I've ever felt.

A small pause as he just looks at her.

I didn't think I would have to tell you all that, spell it out. I thought you would have heard it otherwise.

TIM

You should have told me, you should have told me that freedom meant so much to you.

NORA

But I did tell you, Tim. I told you I didn't want a baby.

There is a very long pause. TIM smiles and begins to chuckle.

What?

TIM laughs harder.

What is so funny about that?

TIM

Nothing.

NORA

You asshole!

TIM

Nothing. I'm sorry. Nothing is... there is nothing funny about
that.

> *He is serious again now.*

I just–

NORA

Asshole.

> *She walks away from him and stands with her back to him.*
> *A pause.*

TIM

Now we don't talk? Now we sit on wet grass. In cold fog. In
pitch black and we don't talk.

NORA

There was nothing funny about that.

TIM

I know.

NORA

We have a problem, Tim, a problem that in six months will have
a face and a name and even more problematic is the fact that
I don't know if I am ready for it. There is nothing funny here.

TIM

I know.

NORA

Then why did you laugh?

TIM

I don't know.

> *Pause.*

Tell me about your mom.

NORA

Fuck you. It's not that easy.

TIM

Nora. Look at me.

> *Pause. He suddenly, and violently, screams at her.*

Look at me!

He frightens her and she all but turns in mid air to face him. There is a long silent moment, then NORA's fear very slowly softens and neutralizes. TIM stares at her intently. He eventually smiles and speaks very softly.

Tell me about your mom.

NORA
She.

TIM
Yes?

NORA conjures a weak smile.

NORA
She would have liked you.

TIM moves towards her.

TIM
You hungry?

NORA
Yeah.

TIM
Just breath mints, huh?

NORA
And cigarettes.

TIM
I'll go find something.

NORA
No.

TIM
I won't go far.

NORA
No, we, we're already lost. I don't want to be out here alone.

TIM
I know. That's why I'm here.

NORA
Tim, please.

TIM
It will be all right.

NORA

We're in the middle of... there's nothing out here.

TIM

Maybe some berries or something.

NORA

Tim–

TIM

Look why don't you stay here and... and tell me a story about your mother. Really loud. Fog can hide the stars but it can't hide your voice. I'll know where you are every second. Okay?

NORA

Okay.

TIM

Okay.

NORA

But you won't go far.

TIM

Wouldn't dream of it.

NORA

Okay.

TIM begins to walk towards the trees.

TIM

So tell me about your mom.

NORA

Well, she would have liked you. Because. Because you watch out for me.

TIM is engulfed by the dark trees. No sight of him. No sound.

And because you look like my dad. My dad when he was young. When they lived here. And all their pictures were soft and out of focus. Like they lived under water.

She removes the little photo from her coat pocket. Throughout the following she slowly forgets that she is talking to TIM and she becomes quiet and more intimate.

And Dad was always smiling and Mom was always smoking. And Aunt Shirley was barely fifteen. And they all lived here, and Mom was still at Grandpa's on the hill. And everyone knew them, knew the family because of their work with the church, and because Grandpa worked with the union. Mom used to show me pictures when she got homesick. Like she needed someone to see them with her to deaden the pain a bit. Dad called her a romantic, and said the entire island smelled like death. He said she would remember that if she ever went back. But she never did. She never brought me here. And then she died and they didn't even bury her here. Buried her in Cambridge. Even though her parents, all her family, were buried down here, they buried her in Cambridge. Said it was for the best. Said it was what she would have wanted. But I don't believe that. I don't believe that's what she would have wanted. I don't believe she hated this place like Dad did. I don't believe she ran away from it. I don't believe she did what everyone thought she did.

There is a small silent pause.

I believe she wanted to have children. And grandchildren.

There is another flash of light. The entire space is washed for a split second and then darkness again. NORA's eyes once again are burned.

Tim!

TIM
I wasn't far.

TIM emerges from the trees very close to NORA. He stands and stares at her.

What?

She is silent. Rubbing her eyes.

What?

NORA
Nothing.

TIM
You call out to me like that. Like you're on fire or something. And nothing.

NORA
I don't want you to leave me again. Okay? Not while we are in here. Not for a second.

TIM
I won't. You okay?

NORA
Yeah.

TIM
Headache?

NORA
Yeah. A little. I just. I guess I got a scare and...

TIM
You got a scare?

NORA
I don't want to feel like that again.

TIM
Like?

NORA
Alone. Stupid. Crazy.

TIM
You're not.

NORA
You're trying hard to sound convinced.

TIM
You are not crazy. And you are definitely not alone.

NORA
As long as you don't leave me.

TIM
No. What you are is hungry.

He opens his hands over her head and plump blueberries rain down on her.

NORA
Tim! Where did you find these? Stop it, you're losing them.

TIM
Plenty more where they came from. We are surrounded.

NORA
Oh, my God, they're beautiful.

TIM
You like?

NORA
Very much. Hmmm. Thank you. You always know how to make me feel better. Or at least forget. Thanks.

She smiles and moves to kiss him. He shifts away.

TIM
You want more?

NORA
No, my God. I'm going to make myself sick on these. Blueberries?

TIM
Yeah.

NORA
Weird time of year for them. Mom used to go berry picking in the late summer. Used to always say they were best just before the first frost.

TIM
Cold enough for it tonight.

NORA
These are months early.

TIM
We shouldn't complain. The earth has offered us her bounty without which we would be stuck with breath mints.

NORA
My God, they're amazing.

TIM
Stick out your tongue.

NORA
No.

TIM
No?

NORA
Come closer.

TIM
Closer?

NORA
Closer.

TIM
Is this good?

NORA
Closer.

> *He is very close. She opens her mouth and shows him her tongue.*

Purple?

> *TIM nods. She giggles.*

You.

> *TIM smiles and slowly opens his mouth. NORA thinks she hears something.*

What was that?

> *Their lights scan the woods. There is a pause and perfect silence.*

Did you hear that?

TIM
Something. Animal. Squirrel or something.

NORA
What is that smell?

TIM
Smell?

NORA
God. Do you smell that? Like something's dead. God.

TIM
I don't know.

NORA
We must be near a sewer or something. Wind changed direction or something. Just out of nowhere.

TIM
Do you still smell it?

NORA
Unless whatever made that noise...

TIM
You are only frightening yourself.

NORA
It's gone again. Just like that.

TIM sees the small picture in her hand.

TIM
You looking at pictures?

NORA
I never smelled anything like that before.

TIM
Forget about it.

NORA
Tim.

TIM
Forget about it.

NORA
I frustrate you, don't I?

TIM
Show me your pretty picture.

NORA
I do frustrate you. You lose your patience.

TIM
Do I?

NORA
Yes, you lose your patience and look at me that way.

TIM
And what way is that?

NORA
Like you're sharing a joke with a part of me I've forgotten. Like I'm crazy.

TIM
Show me your picture.

NORA
I don't blame you for that. It was just an observation.

TIM
Nora. If my gaze bothers you, divert it. Show me the picture.

NORA
You've seen this one.

TIM
I want to see it again.

NORA
Practically had to beg you to sit with me the first time. Remember that? Looking through the albums.

TIM
I don't recall.

NORA
You didn't want to see them then.

TIM
Well, I wasn't sitting in the woods hunting for clues. Show me.

NORA
No clues. Just smiles.

TIM
Let's look.

NORA
Shot of Mom and Dad. Before they moved.

TIM looks at photo. A small pause.

TIM
Your mother.

NORA
You remember?

TIM
What?

NORA
This picture, remember I showed it to you, and my baby pictures? Remember?

TIM
It's coming back to me. She was beautiful.

NORA
She was, wasn't she.

TIM
You okay?

NORA
Yeah. I just. I just become painfully aware sometimes you know. Looking at the photos, talking about her. I have these flashes of

what I've missed. I get these aches. Stupid little aches for her
voice. Her hands. Her guidance.

TIM
Her guidance?

NORA
Yeah. Stupid.

TIM
No. No not at all.

NORA
She was beautiful.

TIM
Yeah. You don't look like her.

NORA
Thanks.

TIM
I didn't mean it like that. You just don't look like her.

NORA
I don't know what to say to that, Tim. It can't be a compliment,
no matter how much you twist it.

TIM
You just look different. Hair. Eyes.

NORA
Better quit while you're ahead.

TIM
That black dress. I mean you would never be caught dead in a
dress like that, would you?

NORA
I don't know.

TIM
Really?

NORA
Mom loved that dress. I remember it, you know. She kept it in
plastic at the back of her closet. Brought it to Cambridge with
her. Couldn't part with it.

TIM
Special significance?

NORA
Who knows.

TIM
Maybe she wore it in here.

A small pause.

Nora?

There is a pause.

Nora?

NORA
I don't want to look at pictures anymore.

TIM
Are you okay?

NORA
I don't know.

TIM
Nora?

NORA
I don't want to look at pictures anymore.

TIM
What is wrong with you?

NORA
I'm freaking myself out. That's what you said, isn't it? Letting my
mind run away with me?

TIM
Tell me.

A small pause.

Nora. Tell me.

NORA
That dress, Tim. She might have, what if she did wear it in here?

TIM
I don't know.

NORA
What if she was wearing it in here?

TIM
Because it was wrapped in plastic in her closet?

NORA
Because she brought it to Cambridge. She never threw it out. She threw most of her stuff out. Landed in Ontario with a single bag.

TIM
Nora–

NORA
That's why they didn't see it at first. The blood. That's why they didn't see the blood until they got her back to town.

TIM
You don't know this.

NORA
Dad said she was covered in blood. Said they saw it all over her face and hands, but they never saw the rest of it until, never noticed it until they got her back to town.

TIM
Nora calm down.

NORA
She was wearing black. In here. In the middle of the woods.

TIM
So she might have worn black.

NORA
In the middle of the woods. She...

 A slight pause.

TIM
She, what?

 Slight pause.

NORA
She didn't want to be found.

TIM
Really.

NORA
Whatever she was doing in here, she didn't want to be found.

TIM
I wouldn't assume that.

NORA
It makes sense, Tim. Think about it.

TIM
I have. She was wearing black, in the middle of the woods, in the middle of the night. So maybe, yeah maybe she didn't want to be found. But Nora. You're wearing black. Your coat.

They look at each other.

You're in the woods in the middle of the night. The question is, really, what does that mean?

A pause.

NORA
I. I don't know.

A longer pause.

TIM
Well, it means that she wasn't dragged in here. She wasn't here against her will.

NORA
I guess.

TIM
That's good news.

NORA
She came in here of her own free will.

TIM
Just like you. Whatever happened after that, well.

NORA is very quiet.

Come here. Sit down.

NORA
I don't want to.

TIM
You must be tired?

NORA
I'm not tired!

TIM
Nora–

NORA
Why did you want to come?

TIM
I told you.

NORA
No, you didn't. Why did you want to come?

TIM
I was concerned.

NORA
What?

TIM
I had concerns.

NORA
Yeah?

TIM
Yes.

NORA
I never... I never thought I would... I wouldn't expect you to worry.

TIM
I was afraid that something would happen. Something like this.

NORA
Do you mean that?

TIM
Yes.

NORA
I asked you for some time Tim, I asked to come do this by myself. And you stood in the airport and told me, told me that either you were coming with me or I shouldn't bother to come back. That I would be on my own. I remember that. How it stung.

TIM
I can't let you wander here alone.

NORA

You said horrible things to me, Tim.... You called me questionable. You said my, my state of mind was questionable. Too questionable to be trusted, to travel alone, too questionable to come here. You remember that?

TIM is staring at her. She turns away from him.

You said that Tim.

TIM

Nora. You could be alone out here. Nora. Nora.

She looks at him again. A pause as he give her a cautionary stare. Her anger dissipates.

Aren't you happy I'm here?

A small pause. She smiles.

NORA

I am. I am happy you're here. I would miss you if you weren't. I'd be carving your face in the trees. Drawing you in the mud.

TIM

Good.

NORA

I'm. Sorry. I know, Tim, I know you deserve better. I don't question that. I've lied to you. You don't deserve it. You lose your temper, say things, do things, but, who could blame you. Tim? I never told you that. That, you deserve better. I love you, Tim.

He smiles.

Did you hear me? I said I love you.

He continues to smile.

Tim?

TIM

I heard you.

A pause.

NORA

In the morning we'll find our way. Know where we are. Right? We can relax then.

TIM
You want this night to end? All this beauty?

NORA
And if not, even if not, they'll look for us. At the gas station. They know we are in here. So.

TIM
Three days worth of beauty, Nora. You want it to end?

NORA
I've told you.

TIM
You want to jump to the end.

NORA
Tim. I'm not leaving without an answer. Even if they come looking. I can't. No more secrets.

TIM
There will always be secrets. You can't know everything.

NORA
I don't want to know everything. I just want to know this.

TIM
Even if you are not meant to?

NORA
Who decides that? Jesus, I told you. I told you how much this meant to me and still you fight me.

TIM
I'm not fighting you. Stay as long as you like. Really. I won't fight you on that.

NORA
But you have, Tim. You have been fighting me.

TIM
I was protecting you.

NORA
Protecting me?

TIM
I was.

NORA
Gee thanks Tim. From what?

TIM
Persistence. It can kill.

NORA
Kill?

TIM
Or maim.

NORA
I'll learn to fear it.

TIM
You couldn't possibly.

NORA
Now, why is that?

TIM
Too late.

NORA
Are you trying to scare me now?

TIM
You are crippled. You know that?

NORA
No, Tim. Tell me.

TIM
Your persistence has crippled you. You are your own enemy.

NORA
Isn't everybody?

TIM
Not everybody closes their eyes and looks for cliffs.

NORA
My eyes are open.

TIM
Having considered the options of what may have happened in here, having thought about this until you are ready to faint, what would you say is the most horrific notion that has presented itself?

NORA
What?

TIM
Go deep inside now.

NORA
No. I don't want to do this.

TIM
Because you see after a really, really, long time conducting field research I have developed a theory.

NORA
A theory.

TIM
People don't search for answers.

NORA
What?

TIM
People don't search for answers. It's not what they want.

NORA
Really?

TIM
Yes. They search for peace. Isn't that what you said?

NORA
I didn't say that, like that.

TIM
And they don't search for peace from questions, for relief from questions, from beautiful tantalizing mysteries.

NORA
I want–

TIM
Answers. They search for peace from answers. From what they know. Answers. You have them.

NORA
Tim.

TIM
So what I would like to ask is... what is so horrible, Nora? What little germ of an idea is so horrible that you had to come all the way down here to destroy it. To prove it wrong.

NORA

I don't want to do this.

TIM

What was she doing in here Nora? What was she doing in here that was so unforgivable?

NORA

I don't know!

TIM

And why would you care? What she was doing. She made it out all right. A little worse for wear but–

NORA

She was my mother, Tim.

TIM

She was a lot of things, wasn't she. Guidance? A role model. A positive example to live by. But, I wonder Nora, what if she set a bad one, a bad example. Then what does that make her? A family embarrassment? Or an excuse?

NORA

Don't, Tim.

TIM

An excuse. Permission. Is that what you were looking for?

NORA

I want to know what really happened.

TIM

I think you might already. That old love heart. Where ever it may be. Very romantic.

NORA

I really saw it, Tim.

TIM

I don't doubt it. This place. So secluded yet impossibly close. Perfect for young love. Mom and Dad in the bushes. Or Mom and someone.

NORA

Don't say that.

TIM

What do you think they were doing in here?

NORA
>Tim, stop it.

TIM
>Just think, you could have been conceived in here.

NORA
>That's not possible.

TIM
>Well, someone could have. Someone could have been conceived in here. It's possible. Likely even.

NORA
>Just stop.

TIM
>Someone could have been conceived in here. Someone could have seen their beginning here.

NORA
>Tim. Please.

TIM
>And?

NORA
>No.

TIM
>And their end.

>*There is a pause.*

NORA
>That is not why.

TIM
>She was covered in blood. She was in here by choice.

NORA
>No, Tim!

TIM
>You said so yourself.

NORA
>I didn't mean that–

TIM
> She was in here by choice. For three days she was in here.
> Dressed in black. Hiding. Plotting. They find her covered in
> blood.

NORA
> That is not what happened!

TIM
> She gets married, she moves away. She never comes back. Adopts
> a child because she can't have one of her own.

NORA
> Fuck you!

TIM
> It's what you came here to disprove.

NORA
> She would not do that!

TIM
> Or prove.

NORA
> She would not do that!

TIM
> But what if she did, Nora?
>
> *There is a pause.*
>
> What does that mean for you?
>
> *Pause.*
>
> What does that mean for you, Nora?

NORA
> I...

TIM
> Permission?

NORA
> I. Don't know.
>
> *She looks at him.*
>
> I don't know.

TIM
> No. You don't.

There is a pause. He walks away from her.

NORA

When I was twelve, a kid in Cambridge told me my mother was evil. That my real mom had been taken. That the woman I knew as my mother was the devil's work. And that she couldn't have kids for my dad. That I was adopted. I remember I ran home and cried and cried. And my Aunt Shirley found me. And I told her what the kid had said and I asked her if I was adopted. If all that was true. And she told me, she told me that Mom was a young woman at the time, and sometimes young women get into trouble. They have special problems that they need time alone to solve. That that was why my mom was in the woods. To solve a problem. I didn't quite understand, but I knew enough not to ask twice. I guess, I forgot that. I forgot that. Until I had a problem of my own.

TIM

And here we are.

NORA

I am lost, Tim. I've been lost for so long, I can't even remember what it's like. To make a decision on my own. To not... depend... on you. And I never felt, I never did feel that she could tell me anything, you know. Offer. Guidance. Until now. How stupid is that?

There is a pause.

TIM

So what do you think? Answers really what you wanted? Or was it that ever elusive peace of mind?

NORA

I don't know what I was hoping to find.

TIM

Really?

NORA

A motive. Maybe. I don't even know why she did it. Why there wasn't a better option.

TIM

Who knows what her circumstances might have been. Why bother with motives when you've got your answers.

NORA

I wish there were better answers.

TIM
Yeah? What would you do with them?

NORA
Publicize them. Broadcast them. Take them out of here kicking and screaming.

TIM
Kicking and screaming?

NORA
I wish there were little people. Goddamn fairies. Hell of a lot more concrete, more immediate than thirty-year-old motives. Easier to grab.

TIM
Easier to handle?

NORA
Easier to explain.

TIM
Easier to explain than Mom mutilating herself in the bush.

She stares at him in disbelief. There is a pause.

Well. That's what she did.

NORA
Fuck you.

TIM
I wonder how she did it?

NORA
Tim–

TIM
Those dainty little berries. Or the nasty stick. Not pleasant.

NORA
Jesus, Tim.

TIM
What?

NORA
You are inhuman sometimes.

TIM
I get told that a lot.

NORA

You're such a... God I forget you know, I forget what it is that you are.

TIM

I'm sorry to disappoint.

NORA

You enjoyed that, pushing me like that, you've enjoyed all of this.

TIM

Immensely.

NORA

Why?

TIM

I'm here for the entertainment.

NORA

You're just trying to hurt me. That's all you've ever tried to do.

TIM

Is it?

NORA

Come here to protect me. You never came here to protect me. You say that, you always say that, for my protection, and then you become the greatest threat.

TIM

I never knew that about myself.

NORA

It was always that way. You can't deny that. There was always a bigger part of you that hated my guts.

TIM

I deny nothing.

NORA

So where does that leave me? You think I can look at you and see a future, see a father?

TIM

You have to look closer. What do you see now?

NORA

You are a waste, Tim.

TIM
> Your words are very strong.

> *She throws her flashlight at him. She is still lit by him, but he is in darkness.*

NORA
> You are a waste and I am not afraid of you.

TIM
> Nora.

NORA
> Standing there like we're talking about the goddamn weather.

> *TIM bends and picks up NORA's light at his feet.*

TIM
> Save your strength.

NORA
> Why are you doing this?

TIM
> Because you have to be punished now.

> *He turns off NORA's light. There is a small pause and then NORA responds weakly like a frightened child.*

NORA
> What?

TIM
> Trespassing.

> *She becomes disoriented.*

NORA
> Fuck you.

TIM
> I politely asked you to leave. Suggested that you do so.

NORA
> You should have just kept walking, Tim. You should have just walked right out of the airport. You should have never come.

TIM
> Nor you, Nora.

NORA
> You should have never gotten on that plane. You should–

TIM
What? What should I not have done?

NORA
Never gotten on that plane.

TIM
Yes?

NORA
You should have just left. While I watched you. While I stood in the check-in line and watched you. Drive away. Not get on the plane. You. You didn't get on the plane.

TIM
Nora?

NORA
My head hurts.

TIM
Are you all right?

NORA
I'm so tired.

TIM
You've had a rough couple of days.

NORA
Tired. You.

TIM
Wet ground. Chill in the air.

NORA
You didn't get on the plane.

TIM
All that talking.

NORA
I came here alone.

> *They stand and face each other. There is a very long pause.*

TIM
Yeah.

> *NORA begins to back away.*

Oh, my. So much indecision, and woe.

NORA
I am not lost. I am not lost anymore.

> *TIM flicks his flashlight off and on. NORA continues to back up.*

TIM
You want me to follow?

NORA
Oh my God.

TIM
Come closer? Closer.

> *He continues to slowly flick his flashlight. TIM stands his ground staring at her. The trees around them begin to shake.*

Closer?

NORA
I'm not afraid of you. I know what you are.

TIM
Closer?

NORA
I know what to do.

TIM
And you're not lost. Right? As long as you can see the stars, you are not lost.

NORA
I am not lost!

TIM
You know exactly where you are.

NORA
I am not lost!

> *TIM opens his mouth and breathes loudly. NORA coughs loudly. His light dies. There is complete darkness. The trees are shaking furiously now. We hear NORA coughing and moving. Throughout the following the trees shake and create waves of noise, loud then quiet.*

I can't breathe. The smell. It hurts. It hurts! Oh God it hurts it hurts it hurts. No. I won't, I won't shout. Don't be afraid. No. Don't be afraid. Don't be afraid don't be afraid don't be afraid don't be afraid. I'm not afraid anymore. No. I can't see the stars anymore, I can't, but I'm not afraid. It's over. It's over and I'm not afraid.

There is another brilliant flash of light that reveals NORA lying on her back on her blanket. Her coat is closed around her as if she were freezing. Her hands rest on her stomach. The trees are completely still and the river cannot be heard. Perfect silence. She stares weakly at the sky and smiles.

Daylight.

The sunlight starts to fade. She notices it. She moves a hand to her forehead to brush hair out of her eyes. Her fingers leave bright red trails of blood on her face. She notices this and looks at her hands. She opens her coat. The legs and belly of her clothes beneath are soaked with blood. Lights fade very slowly throughout the following. She speaks calmly and softly.

Oh Nora. Look at you. What will people think? And what will you tell them? I don't know. I'll, I'll tell them I don't know anything. I don't.

She begins slowly smearing her face and arms with the blood.

I don't know anything about Butler's Marsh. I don't know anything about Butler's Marsh. About Butler's Marsh. About Butler's Marsh. About Butler's Marsh. Butler's Marsh. Butler's Marsh. Butler's Marsh. Butler's Marsh. Butler's Marsh.

Complete darkness again. She continues to chant. Then silence. And darkness that goes on a little too long.

The end.

Tempting Providence

— • — Notes — • —

Like most of my generation, I knew very little about Nurse Bennett when I was approached to write her story. Sadly, I never learned about her in school, and legends of her heroics were isolated to those in the nursing profession, residents of Newfoundland's Great Northern Peninsula, on the province's west coast, and lucky chance visitors to Bennett House in beautiful Daniel's Harbour. Much research filled my desk with Nurse Bennett's 60 years worth of staggering work, 60 years worth of potential material. As I condensed the material I found most of what I was interested in exploring revolved around Myra's first years in Newfoundland, and the awkward transition period between life in London, England, and life in Daniel's Harbour, Newfoundland. Nurse Bennett's records and diaries offered much, but strangely absent from all findings was a solid basis for dramatic conflict. As Angus says, "She was a thoughtful woman, and a private one." As a result, much of what exists in this text in terms of what "she was thinking" is extrapolation. Talk of loneliness and unhappiness are examples of my artistic license, and, though well supported, are fiction.

Tempting Providence was created to be a quickly-paced, simple, and smooth play based upon a story that was anything but; Nurse Bennett's true life story is one hundred years long, and rich in content that was neither simple, nor, most times, smooth. The hope is to illuminate a telling section of this personal history in a way that is not simply biographic, but also highly theatrical.

Tempting Providence was commissioned by Theatre Newfoundland Labrador in 2000, and was premiered at their Gros Morne Theatre Festival in Cow Head, Newfoundland, in June 2002. It was subsequently remounted and co-presented with Artistic Fraud of Newfoundland in St. John's, Newfoundland, in December 2002, with the following company:

MYRA   Deidre Gillard-Rowlings
ANGUS   Daniel Payne
MAN   Peter Rompkey
WOMAN   Melanie Caines

Directed and Design Concept by Jillian Keiley
Stage Managed by Karla Biggin
Set Construction by George Cammie and Walter J. Snow
Lighting Design by Walter J. Snow
Costume Design by Barry Buckle
Production Management by Diana Haynes

The play was again remounted in April 2003 and toured to the National Arts Centre's Atlantic Scene Festival, Ottawa, and to Eastern Front Theatre's On the Waterfront Festival, Dartmouth, Nova Scotia, with the following company:

MYRA   Deidre Gillard-Rowlings
ANGUS   Darryl Hopkins
MAN   Peter Rompkey
WOMAN   Melanie Caines

— • — — • — — • —

This play was truly a community initiative. It was set in motion by the people of Daniel's Harbour and surrounding area, and specifically by members of the Nurse Myra Bennett Foundation. For years they had insisted that the Gros Morne Theatre Festival honour Nurse Bennett with a show. I thank them for their foresight and persistence, and Jeff Pitcher and Gaylene Buckle of Theatre Newfoundland Labrador for listening to them, and thinking of me. I am also deeply indebted to the generosity and support of the Bennett family, and specifically to Trevor, for his enthusiasm, energy, and trust.

—•— Characters —•—

MYRA   Age 31 years at the beginning of the play, which progresses
         through approximately ten years of her life. Stern, though
         caring, serious, though quick witted.

ANGUS   Late twenties at the beginning of the play. Thoughtful,
         playful, charming, down to earth. The perfect man. A
         working man. A warm heart and dirty hands.

MAN   Various distinct male characters, aged fourteen to eighty.

WOMAN   Various distinct female characters, aged nineteen to eighty.

—•— Setting —•—

Stage should be relatively bare, with limited use of props and
costumes. The play is actor-driven. Myra and Angus are constant
characters. Man and Woman denote a variety of characters which
become self evident in the dialogue and minor stage directions. It
is strongly recommended that these characters themselves be actor-
driven, and not be reliant on costuming.

All actors should remain on stage unless otherwise noted. While
not in a given scene they should be visible giving focus to the action.
It may be desired to have Myra and Angus in constant character, even
when not in scene. May and Woman may be omnipotent, and at times
become watchers of the event.

Set and time change should be executed primarily with lighting, if
at all. The play is written to move quickly and swiftly through scenes.
The text does the work. Pause should only be taken where noted. Fun,
fast, playful, and, above all, theatrical.

TEMPTING PROVIDENCE

— • — Act One — • —

ANGUS alone.

ANGUS
Who knows the answer to that? A person's inner thoughts like
that. It's a forbidden domain. She was a thoughtful woman, and
a private one. So, as for what she was thinking, what was on her
mind, who can say. I don't pretend to know everything. Why she
decided to stay, was content to stay. Put down roots here, of all
places. Here.

MYRA stares out to sea.

MYRA
Daniel's Harbour.

ANGUS
Smack in the middle of three hundred miles of sparsely occupied
coast. Daniel's Harbour.

MYRA
Though there is really no harbour at all. The sharp land as
straight and fierce as the long horizon that it dutifully stares
down. A collection of houses sit at the top, where the grass
begins. A collection of people in front of them. Waiting. I am
late. What a horrible way to make a first impression. Three
weeks late but only as a result of the ungovernable will of God.
Pack ice so thick, and a late spring thaw has meant that my
passage north was to be late beyond being fashionable. The
stranger arrives to the strange land. On the *SS Home*.

A weak smile.

The *Home* carries the first provisions the area has seen since
autumn. People scramble for the food first, and then later to me
for introductions. A long thin hand falls into mine and it's loose
skin, it's thinness makes me recall that of my grandmother's. A
comforting thought on my first day here if not for the fact that
this dainty hand is attached to the arm of a forty-year-old man.
Many are sick. They will not tell you such, but it is clear enough.
Many near starvation. It takes little of my formal experience and

training to identify why I have been placed here. It takes no time at all to see a most urgent need for a nurse.

MAN and WOMAN enter.

WOMAN
Well, she insisted, you see.

MAN
Yes, insisted.

WOMAN
From the very first day. First time she stepped her foot off the boat.

MAN
And there were some...

WOMAN
Oh there were.

MAN
That were none too delighted to be told that, to be commanded right?

WOMAN
And that's what she did too. Commanded, yes sir.

MAN
No sir, there were some that needed to be told twice, but few a third time, and even fewer a fourth.

WOMAN
You just didn't cross her. Not when she made her wishes known.

MAN
No, not when she made her wishes known.

WOMAN
She was a strong woman.

MAN
Strong, powerful woman.

WOMAN
A strong woman, so you listened.

MAN
You listened all right.

WOMAN
You listened to what she told you.

MYRA
You will refer to me as Nurse. Nurse. Nurse Grimsley if you prefer, but never Miss. And certainly not Mrs. I would demand your respect just as I'm sure that you would expect to have mine. I will be seeing patients as soon as humanly possible. I trust you all know where to find me.

ANGUS
I don't think she even knew where she was staying at that point. The minister had her all set up over at George Moss' place. School teacher at the time. Now George's place wasn't big sir, by no stretch, but they did manage to find her room in the parlour for a nice little clinic, and the patients, they were to wait in the kitchen. Well, that's the way it was. She landed and she was hardly unpacked before people were over with every ailment under the sun. A good few of them simply there to meet her, check her out. People were just glad she was finally here, glad to finally have a nurse. And I guess I counted among them.

WOMAN enters and stares at MYRA.

MYRA
Hello.

No response.

ANGUS
But us, we never met that day.

He steps aside as MYRA approaches the WOMAN.

MYRA
I'm Nurse Grimsley.

No response.

And you are?

No response.

My first patient.

WOMAN
Knows it all, do ya?

MYRA
Pardon me?

WOMAN
Thinks ya knows it all.

MYRA
Well, I've certainly never said that.

WOMAN
Oh yes, you knows it all all right.

MYRA
Perhaps enough to help. What is the trouble?

WOMAN
Where you from?

MYRA
Madam–

WOMAN
Not Newfoundland.

MYRA
No.

WOMAN
Where?

MYRA
I ask the questions. What is the trouble?

WOMAN
Where are you from?

MYRA
None of your business.

WOMAN
You're all up in my face about my troubles.

MYRA
And the day I come to your place of work, where you have set
aside some of your time to speak to me about where I am from,
where I originate, then that day, madam, you shall know every
last detail of my history and upbringing, but as long as you walk
through my door, as long as you stand in my place of work, I will
ask the questions, and I will refuse to be apologetic about it or
my personal privacy.

> *A short pause. The WOMAN starts a slow chuckle that turns into
> a laugh.*

WOMAN
You're all right.

MYRA
Thank you.

WOMAN
Pain in my hip.

MYRA
Well good. Not your pain, but your co-operation.

WOMAN
Some tongue on you.

MYRA
Yes, well, I apologize.

WOMAN
No girl. Good to hear. Good to hear. Good to have another one like myself around.

MYRA
Yes. Okay.

WOMAN
That what it takes?

MYRA
Pardon me?

WOMAN
I have to invite you over to my place of work, set aside some time to find out where you're from?

MYRA
What if I said yes?

WOMAN
I'd have to invite you over for tea then wouldn't I?

MYRA
Why, yes, I suppose you would.

WOMAN
Well, that's it then.

MYRA
Yes, I suppose it is. Mrs?

WOMAN
House. Ow. Yeah that's it right there.

MYRA alone.

MYRA
There is a cautious curiosity here. I must remember that. I must remember that these people, not only have they never had any formal medical aid, but they also rarely meet someone new. I am standing in front of Mrs. House's, and I am watched by my new neighbours. They look at me from the paths. They whisper as they walk. They exist in this sublime world of friends and relatives. So, of course, there will be a trust issue, with a stranger in town. A stranger barking commands. And this is fine. I'm not here to make friends. That is not my intent. I must remember that too. As I knock on this door. As I start to talk pleasantries.

MYRA at Mrs. House's for tea.

WOMAN
What difference does it make?

MYRA
Honestly I don't know. But my mother would have it no other way.

WOMAN
Foolishness really. It is.

MYRA
There is a difference in the taste. It's noticeable.

WOMAN
Just because you put the milk in first? Tea is tea is tea, my dear.

MYRA
Call it a habit then.

WOMAN
We all got them. Habits. You might be having to break some of yours.

MYRA
I'll just start some new ones. You're smiling.

WOMAN
Lovely accent girl. It is. Not polite to say that I suppose.

MYRA releases a small tight smile.

You bake?

MYRA
Bake?

WOMAN
Bread.

MYRA
I've never had much occasion to.

WOMAN
Now see. That's gonna change.

MYRA
Is it.

WOMAN
Got to. You got to bake. No self respecting woman on this coast that don't bake. Sew. Knit.

MYRA
Really.

WOMAN
Yes. The crowd around here won't be paying you no mind with your do this and don't do that if they finds out you can't even do that stuff. I can hear Wallace Carter now. Yes now, go and see her, have her mend my body when she can't even mend a pair of socks.

MYRA
So, I've got some learning to do?

WOMAN
Yes girl, women round here got skills, do anything. Knit a house they could. Predict the weather.

MYRA
Soothsayers too eh?

WOMAN
Not all, no. But some girl. Some of them are right spooky. There's a few of them on this coast, can tell, just by looking at you, if you're with child.

MYRA smiles.

It's true as I'm sitting here. Tell a young one she's pregnant before she even knows herself.

MYRA
Do you believe that?

WOMAN

Some of them. I tell ya. Lean over the table and say, do you know you're pregnant? Just like that.

MYRA

And they are always correct?

Mrs. House smiles.

WOMAN

Well who can say eh? No one really keeps track of who said what and when and who was right or no. But, you'll come to see all that yourself by and by. You'll come to see that all soon enough. Break a few habits. Make a few new ones. Fit right in eh?

MYRA

Learn to bake. Knit a house.

WOMAN

Don't go worrying about that. I can help you out with that stuff easy enough. You'll be a good hand at it all when I'm done with ya.

MYRA gives a small smile.

MYRA

I believe it.

ANGUS alone.

ANGUS

There was nothing much to speak of. At first. And it's hardly my story. But if you want to know the facts of it. Where I was, where she was. The circumstances of us being in the same place at the same time. The series of events that caused her to be shaking my hand. For her to be in my house. For Alex to have gone and fetched her.

MYRA alone. MAN enters.

MAN

Nurse?

MYRA

Yes.

MAN

You busy?

MYRA

I make a point to always be busy sir. I haven't met you.

MAN

Alex, ma'am. Alex Bennett.

MYRA

Yes Alex Bennett, how may I help you?

MAN

I don't mean to disturb.

MYRA

Not at all. Just beginning some baking. I've been feeling the need to diversify my talents while here. Do you bake?

MAN

No ma'am.

MYRA

I'm led to believe that it may not be good enough to just be a nurse on this coast. I'm led to believe that any woman worth her weight can bake a batch of bread and darn a pair of socks. Do you believe that Alex Bennett?

MAN

I don't know ma'am.

MYRA

Could you refer to me as Nurse please, Mr. Bennett. I applaud your formality, but when it comes out of your mouth as ma'am it makes me feel much older than my years demand.

MAN

Yes, ma'am. Nurse.

MYRA

Are you sick Mr. Bennett?

MAN

Me? Oh no.

MYRA

I see. Well?

MAN

Yes?

MYRA

To what do I owe the pleasure?

MAN

Oh, my mother. She's having a baby?

MYRA
Yes?

MAN
Uh, now.

MYRA
Now? She's in labour?

MAN
I'm no doctor but–

MYRA
But she's in pain, she is sweating and crying? Swearing?

MAN
Yeah.

MYRA
And how long were we going to discuss the weather Mr. Bennett?

> *She frantically collects her supplies and washes her bread-making hands.*

Lessons learned, remember this. They are a charming people. They will give you the clothes off their back. They will sleep on the floor as to give you their beds. Their last piece of bread will be yours sooner than theirs. They are as kind and gentle and welcoming as any group you will ever encounter. They are good. And they will panic over a toothache as though it is the mark of death itself, and they will suffer through racking coughs and chest pains rather than seek medical advice. And they will saunter, oh yes, take their bloody sweet time, to collect the nurse for a mother and child as close to parting ways as the bubbling red sea.

> *She runs into the Bennett House.*

ANGUS
She came running through the door with Alex.

MYRA
Where?

MAN
Just in here.

ANGUS
Ran right past me. Don't even think she saw me.

MYRA

Mrs. Bennett? How are you today ma'am?

WOMAN

Oh, girl, I've been better.

ANGUS

There was a formality to her step, the very speed at which she walked that demanded respect. That made you not only feel obliged to give it, but happy to do so.

MYRA

Alex?

MAN

Yes Nurse?

MYRA

Get out.

MAN

Ma'am? Nurse?

MYRA

It is your home, and normally I would never dare, but I must insist that you both leave. Your mother and I would prefer to be alone. I hope I don't speak out of turn Mrs. Bennett.

WOMAN

Alex get out. Take Angus with you.

MAN

Yes, ma'am.

ANGUS

And that was that. Hardly a word spoken and she had myself and Alex out. Feet scraping on the porch. Ears perked to hear over the wind. The scatter noise from behind that fat door and our mother in labour. Our mother in labour and our hands in our pockets. Wearing a path with unlaced boots and not so much as a sweater. But we didn't get back in that house sir until Nurse saw fit. And when we finally walked through the door, here was this sight you know. Mom with little Margaret. And this woman. She was walking slower. Her hands and mouth not moving as fast. She was off duty see. All done. And it was then that she took the time, and only then, to shake my hand.

MAN

Nurse, Nurse this is my brother Angus.

MYRA
Mr. Bennett.

ANGUS
Nurse.

They shake hands. They continue to shake hands through the following.

MYRA
I've only signed on for two years, after two years who knows where I will be. I've come here to help people. I've come here to be of assistance. I have found myself a place of respect, with these people, with this town. I have done good work. I truly believe that. I have taught people, I have saved lives. I have just delivered my first baby in this town. My second since arriving on this coast. That, that is why I am here. Not this hand. Not this arm, and shoulder. Not this.

They stop shaking hands.

Some fresh bedding and a pot of tea please Mr. Bennett.

She returns to Mrs. Bennett. ANGUS remains staring at her.

ANGUS
That's all. There was just nothing much to speak of. In that other way. She was all about the work. There was nothing much happening within her but that. Work. Not then. Not when we first met. That was going to be up to me to change.

MYRA at Mrs. House's for tea.

WOMAN
You like it here?

MYRA
I've only been but six months. Too early to say.

WOMAN
I ask cause, this crowd, the crowd around here can give a bad first impression. Don't mind them though. Give you the shirt off their backs.

MYRA
I have no doubt.

WOMAN
How long do you plan to stay?

MYRA
I've signed on for two years. That's all the budget will allow for right now.

WOMAN
Not gonna change the world in two years. Not that easy.

MYRA
I'm aware.

WOMAN
Lot of coast here. People are spread out.

MYRA
I'm aware of that too. And it doesn't daunt me in the slightest. It hasn't killed me yet, so.

WOMAN
Well, yes, you'll get back and forth easy enough in summer. Foot paths all up and down the coast. And of course by boat. Fast, easy. But winter my dear. Now that's another story.

MYRA
Ice?

WOMAN
No going by boat then.

MYRA
Foot path then?

WOMAN
You're braver than I my dear. To even be out there in the likes of that come January.

MYRA
I've heard stories of your winter.

WOMAN
They're all true. Every last one of them. The winter here. Long as the coast itself. Cold. Even on the good days, wind coming from the west, and not the North, well sir, she's still whipping across that sea there like there's no tomorrow. Picking up water and salt. Flinging it at ya from October to May. Scaring ya?

MYRA
No roads at all.

WOMAN

No my dear. Be cold day in hell too before the crowd in St. John's sees fit to dump that kind of money on this coast.

MYRA

Well.

WOMAN

Two years eh? Think you'll last that long.

MYRA

I don't know. Think you'll have a road in two years? Can't leave you without a nurse. Without a sensible road. It wouldn't be right.

WOMAN

I'm gonna ask you that question again. In February.

She smiles. MYRA, it would seem, cannot.

ANGUS alone.

ANGUS

It was just a joke. I was up in the woods. When the steamer brought her up back in May. The first sensible day of cutting since the snow had gone. Nice day all around. Saw the boat from the top of the hill on the way back and I slapped Alex right hard on the back. That's the nurse I said. We got ourselves a nurse now. Think I'll marry her.

MYRA on a footpath. Two heavy bags.

MAN

You're the nurse.

MYRA

Correct you are.

MAN

Where you going?

MYRA

Parson's Pond.

She drops one of the bags. He watches her pick it up.

MAN

You walking?

MYRA

That was the plan.

MAN
> Nice ways.

MYRA
> Yes, it has been in the past.

MAN
> Nice day for it though.

MYRA
> How old are you?

MAN
> Fourteen.

MYRA
> Isn't there something you should be doing?

MAN
> Could be. Always could be I suppose.

MYRA
> Well?

MAN
> Well.

> *She gives a disgruntled sigh.*

MYRA
> Goodbye then.

MAN
> Okay.

> *He begins to walk away.*

MYRA
> Were you even going to offer?

MAN
> Pardon.

MYRA
> Assistance. Were you even going to offer, in politeness.

MAN
> Truth be told Nurse, that's why mother sent me down the path. Saw you wobbling under the bags. Thought you could use a hand down the shore.

> *Small pause.*

MYRA
She, did?

MAN
Her express orders. Not to offer. Make yourself be known and if she needs you she'll ask. She said she wouldn't have a fine independent woman like yourself bothered by the likes of me. The nurse made that trip countless times already she said. Don't you dare insult her to even offer to carry a bag. Don't you touch a thing. Unless, you needed the help that is. Asked for it expressly.

MYRA
I see. Well. I'm sorry.

MAN
No, no need for that.

They stand and smile at each other for a moment.

MYRA
Well, you will have to remind me to thank your mother.

She holds one of her bags out for him to take.

MAN
Will do. Good day.

He turns and exits. MYRA stares after him in disbelief, and lets the heavy bag fall to the ground. ANGUS steps in behind her.

ANGUS
Heart's in the right place.

MYRA
Mr. Bennett.

ANGUS
Not the sharpest knife in the drawer but none of his crowd ever were.

MYRA
I suppose. I mean he did mean well.

ANGUS
You going far?

MYRA
Parson's Pond.

ANGUS
Emergency?

MYRA
No. No, nothing terribly urgent.

ANGUS
I shouldn't break our necks in haste then.

MYRA
Excuse me?

ANGUS
Them bags look as heavy as you. Not fit to be carrying by yourself.

MYRA
You don't have to really.

ANGUS
No trouble.

MYRA
Really I would prefer it if you–

ANGUS
You prefer it if I ran back and got that little fella for ya.

A silent standoff.

Well. Good.

MYRA
It's just, very kind, excessively kind of you. I mean it is a long walk.

ANGUS
I knows how long a walk it is. Too long to walk it alone. Should never have to travel alone.

MYRA
I'm quite used to it.

ANGUS
Still doesn't make it right. It's too quiet out here. Gives you a false sense of safety.

MYRA
Am I in danger?

ANGUS
Never said that either, but, you can't be too careful.

MYRA
I've never equated silence with danger Mr. Bennett.

ANGUS
No?

MYRA
Peril wears many masks, but none so pretty as this.

He smiles.

ANGUS
Peril?

MYRA
Excuse me?

ANGUS
You've come face to face then. With danger, peril.

MYRA
Do you think women are immune to ugliness Mr. Bennett?

ANGUS
What, angry patients? Babies screaming in your ears?

MYRA
My first years doing this sort of thing, in England, back in Woking during the great war. Do you know nothing of war?

ANGUS
I know my share. I was a merchant marine.

MYRA
Well then you know enough to know that women still have children, and people get sick and people get hurt. With surprising frequency.

ANGUS
And?

MYRA
And, you go. Regardless. Sirens and blackouts, bombs.

A small pause.

ANGUS
And, you're out in all that. By yourself, walking around.

MYRA
Biking, around.

ANGUS
That's something.

MYRA
Had to be done. Someone is sick, someone is in labour–

ANGUS
You go. Brave woman.

MYRA simply stares at him.

What? I say so.

MYRA
It's not like that. Bravery, it doesn't come into it. You just did it. Can't adequately explain it. I just remember that. No room for fear.

ANGUS
I don't believe that. You're just being humble.

MYRA
Excuse me?

ANGUS
You are.

MYRA
Mr. Bennett, I hardly find it funny.

ANGUS
I didn't–

MYRA
It was an exceptionally odd time, and sensation.

ANGUS
I'm sure–

MYRA
It was near impossible to feel anything at all. Things were so bleak, stripped bare. It was a place and time of action and reaction and little else. You couldn't allow yourself to feel anything, because if you started to cry, or scream, or, or laugh, then you would find yourself never having occasion to stop.

A small pause.

Emotion was, scant. Like there was nothing left to lose. You must think me heartless.

ANGUS
No. No not at all.

MYRA
It. It just was. It just was what it was. And it made me
appreciate, made me see the value of all this. Of quiet walks in
the country.

ANGUS
Yes. I suppose it would.

> *He smiles. A long uncomfortable pause, as they look ahead.*

MYRA
Lovely day. Your country really is quite beautiful.

ANGUS
I still think you shouldn't have to.

> *A pause as she looks at him again. He remains staring ahead.*

Travel alone.

> *She turns back out and smiles in spite of herself.*

> *ANGUS alone.*

I told Alex I was going to marry her. And like I said, it was a
joke. And Alex wasn't going to hold me to it, so I certainly
wasn't thinking much about it. But that day, our first walk, to
hear her talking like that. War and such. It was something. It left
me curious. How many times this woman in front of me had
truly felt afraid. And what forces it would take to inspire it in
her. I was thinking of what good stuff would have to be waiting
in the wings for her to finally have the courage to really feel
something. To be scared. To bawl. To eventually stop. I was
thinking of that, and somehow that joke about courting and
marriage, it wasn't all that much a joke anymore.

> *MYRA with a young male patient and his mother.*

WOMAN
Go on, tell her.

MYRA
Hello to you too.

WOMAN
Go on, tell her, she's a busy woman.

MYRA

Is there a problem?

WOMAN

Fell off the fence. Go on tell her. Tell her you fell off the fence.

MYRA

You fell off a fence?

WOMAN

Fell off the fence, after walking up and down the length of it. Walking up and down the length of it after me going blue in the face for lack of breath for having wasted it on telling you not to go walking up and down the length of it. Go on tell her.

MYRA

Madam–

WOMAN

Go on, tell her where you fell. Tell her.

MAN

Mom.

MYRA

Madam–

WOMAN

Tell her. Blue in the face. Telling him he's gonna ruin himself. Telling him he's gonna ruin himself and what does he go and do. Tell her.

MYRA

Madam–

WOMAN

Walked up and down the fence, walked up and down the fence and fell. Fell and ruined himself no doubt. Ruined himself. Go on tell him. Tell him he ruined himself.

MYRA

Madam! Please, if you would. A second alone with the patient.

WOMAN

Oh that's all right girl, nothing I haven't seen before. Take off your pants Henry.

MYRA

Madam–

WOMAN
Four boys. Four fine boys, nothing I haven't seen before. Go on
Henry take off your pants and show the nurse where you fell on
yourself.

MYRA alone.

MYRA
I'm sure it is bred out of concern. I am sure that it stems from
a maternal instinct so strong, made so strong by the elements,
the harshness of their surroundings. The need to protect,
nurture beyond an age that is more than reasonable. And not
just children. Brothers. Husbands, parents, grandparents. I'm
sure there is a reason why here they are, travelling in packs,
travelling in packs to the Nurse to have their bodies exposed,
examined, picked apart for fault. Their none too delightful
and often embarrassing conditions diagnosed and treated with
extended family in tow. Leaning over my shoulder to get the best
possible look. I'm sure there is a reason for it. But, I'm sorry.
Privacy. If I'm not to have roads, sensible supplies, at least give
me privacy. I demand it for their sake as much as my own.
And yet, they are looking at me with long faces of hurt and
disappointment like I'm spoiling the family picnic. It strikes
me, it strikes me as almost. I'm going to say it. Selfish.

MAN and WOMAN alone.

WOMAN
Painfully clear it was.

MAN
Indeed it was.

WOMAN
Painfully clear to anyone who was looking.

MAN
Looking close enough.

WOMAN
And for us.

MAN
Yes us, we were looking.

WOMAN
And for us it was clear as the nose on your face.

MAN

The nose on your face sir.

WOMAN

He, suddenly all interested in the health care.

MAN

And she ten times as short with him as anyone.

WOMAN

Oh, she'd deny it to this day.

MAN

Of that I'm sure.

WOMAN

Deny it black and blue, to and fro.

MAN

Inside out.

WOMAN

But it was clear.

MAN

Crystal clear.

WOMAN

Clear as what I'm saying to you here. There was something on the go from the start.

MAN

From the very start.

WOMAN

There was something on the go between them two.

MYRA and ANGUS step out on the porch.

MYRA

My lord, it is hot in there.

ANGUS

Is that why we are out here?

MYRA

You people, it's amazing. This perfectly nice house, with a perfectly nice parlour, couches, chairs, and you all insist upon squeezing into a kitchen the size of a closet.

ANGUS

It's a proper dance my dear. Can't stray from the kitchen.

MYRA
Really.

ANGUS
You complaining?

MYRA
What?

ANGUS
You weren't having fun?

MYRA
I simply said it was hot.

ANGUS
Think I didn't notice the circle you were spinning around that room with Alex? Cut a path right into the floorboards no doubt. I told Mother not to invite you, you would only do damage.

MYRA
I didn't say I wasn't enjoying myself Mr. Bennett.

ANGUS
You're just hot.

MYRA
Warm. Yes. Too warm.

ANGUS
Now see that sounds like the words of a woman who is not planning on walking back into that kitchen for one more dance.

MYRA
I honestly don't think I'm up for it.

ANGUS
You are going home after having the last dance with Alex. That's not a slap in the face is it.

MYRA
Your brother was very insistent.

ANGUS
Runs in the family. Just like our dancing. Give me half the chance, I'll prove it.

MYRA
Your insistence?

ANGUS
You're not going home yet.

MYRA
Excuse me?

ANGUS
Unless you want half the town thinking you're only after younger men.

MYRA
Inappropriate, Mr. Bennett.

ANGUS
I agree. Doesn't become you.

MYRA
Stop it. What do I have to say? What would you have me do?

ANGUS
Take five minutes. Long enough to catch your breath.

Another silent standoff. She holds his gaze, and then looks up at the sky.

MYRA
Lovely night. You have a lot of them here.

ANGUS
Yes. I keep forgetting that our beloved nurse has only been with us since the spring. She has not had the pure pleasure of a Newfoundland winter.

MYRA
You all have this big talk about winter. Like it's a terror. You're not frightening me. I don't scare off that easily.

ANGUS
No?

MYRA
I, my dear man, have battled and braved worse foes than your much vilified Newfoundland winter.

ANGUS
So you think.

MYRA
You are so smug Mr. Bennett. How can you be sure that I do not have a fondness for a little snow and wind?

He laughs.

How can you be sure Mr. Bennett that your lengthy winter is not one of the reasons I chose to come to Newfoundland in the first place?

ANGUS
Was it?

MYRA
As a matter of fact, yes.

ANGUS
Our winters and our kitchen parties.

A small pause.

What were your reasons?

MYRA
What?

ANGUS
Why did you come here?

A small pause.

MYRA
No great secret, I wanted to help. I wanted to help people.

ANGUS
Newfoundlanders.

MYRA
Newfoundlanders. Anybody.

ANGUS
Could of helped anybody in England. Didn't need to come all the way over here to do that.

MYRA
It was a question of need. There was a great and saddening need here. I read a story about a family in Saskatchewan. I originally applied to go there. And was told I was needed more here.

ANGUS
One story about one family and you packed up your life?

MYRA
A young mother, her first child. Her and her husband lived quite a distance out. Quite a few days travel to anybody else. He left to get help. Left as soon as they thought the baby might be on its

way. Weather set in. Help was too far away. Hours turn into days. Story has a sad ending.

ANGUS
And that was that? Duty calls?

MYRA
Stories about mothers and babies deserve only the happiest of endings.

A small pause. He smiles at her.

ANGUS
They are all afraid of you you know. Terrified. Gotta do what the Nurse says or else.

She looks at the sky silently.

It just the way you talk to them.

MYRA
It's necessary sometimes, to make myself clear, and listened to.

ANGUS
Oh you don't have to tell me. It's just... I think they see this one side of you. They see this Nurse. A very good Nurse, well respected, don't get me wrong. But they just see that side. And, that's a shame. Because... I get the feeling that Nurse Grimsley has a depth that would make the very Atlantic blush with shame.

She remains staring at the sky.

MYRA
Mr. Bennett–

ANGUS
Your five minutes are up.

She looks at him.

Do you have your breath?

A warm pause.

MYRA
I believe so.

ANGUS
Yes?

MYRA
Take me back to your hot and crowded kitchen. If you must.

ANGUS laughs.

ANGUS
If I must?

MYRA
If you must, take me to your kitchen sir. Dance me until my legs themselves plead for clemency.

Fast dancing and music. ANGUS breaks away.

ANGUS
She stayed for two more hours that night. Only danced with me twice. Danced with every other guy there. With Alex four or five times. Didn't matter though. She could have danced with anyone she pleased. She could have refused me a dance outright. For she smiled at few of them. She talked to even less. And with me, with me she took her five-minute breaks, which stretched to twenty. Empty porch step. Cold colouring our breath. Long talks circling nothing. Stars the only witnesses.

ANGUS joins up with her again. Dancing and music dissolves into MYRA sitting by herself. Tired and slow.

MYRA
My hands and shoulders are very tired. I don't often realize the strain I put on them. It is different with teeth. Pulling teeth. There is less at stake, so you can... more of your mind can wander to your joints and muscles and bones. Take stock of yourself. But, with birthing it is much more involved. So, you don't often realize your own fatigue, pain until everyone else is comfortable. Until the only pain in the room is your own. But today, I walk out of that house, clean myself. Get myself home. Make supper. Sit on my bed, and close my eyes and force it out. And then, then I feel this ache in my arms. Only after all of that. She was crying when I left. The same for Roy. Their first child. And there is no consoling them that there will be more. There's no talk of breach birth, by way of explanation, of umbilical cords, of suffocation. There is no explanation. There is no consoling. You just leave, and clean yourself, and make supper. And then, only then, do your arms hurt.

MYRA walking alone.

WOMAN
Good day Nurse.

MYRA
> Good day...

WOMAN
> Mary.

MYRA
> Mary, yes. Forgive me. How are things today?

WOMAN
> Good, Nurse. Killing my back, but good.

MYRA
> Potatoes?

WOMAN
> Turnip. Bit of cabbage over there. Next spring gonna plant more potatoes though. Never puts down enough. Says it every year. Never learn.

MYRA
> Hard work.

WOMAN
> All hard work on this coast. Nobody gets it easy. I would say especially yourself.

MYRA
> Normally I'd feign humility, but these past days.

WOMAN
> Dorothy Walsh. Tough going.

MYRA
> This is a very small town, isn't it.

WOMAN
> How is she?

MYRA
> Surviving.

WOMAN
> Poor soul. Her first too eh?

MYRA
> It was a hard day. Dorothy had it hard.

WOMAN
> Like I told ya. All hard work on this coast.

MYRA
It's true, isn't it. You can't do anything easily.

WOMAN
Would if I could. But most times you don't even get the option. Feet out first? Dorothy? Breach is it you calls it?

MYRA
She had it hard.

WOMAN
My mother, the very same.

MYRA
Yes?

WOMAN
And my sister-in-law. A bugger of time, both of them had.

MYRA
It's as common as the grass it would seem. I've never seen the like. And I'm completely at a loss.

WOMAN
Good Lord got a weird sense of humour when it comes to this place Nurse. Summer, land of milk and honey and beautiful sun and sea. Winter, a slap in the face for six months. Same with everything else. The most beautiful babies in the world. And the labour that hard to almost make it not worthwhile.

MYRA
All hard work on this coast.

WOMAN
You better believe it.

MYRA
Better let you get back to yours.

WOMAN
Good day to you.

MYRA
Yes Mary, take care.

She begins to leave.

WOMAN
Nurse.

MYRA
Yes.

WOMAN
Regardless of how hard it was, the birthing I mean. It was worse before. You know that right? It was all much worse before you got here.

A small pause and a weak smile.

MYRA
I'll take some of those turnip if you're willing to sell.

WOMAN
Always willing.

MYRA alone.

MYRA
It is a crisp night in late September. The summer is almost gone now. The fall itself will not last long I am told. The air feels thick in my lungs. Thick with water and cold. Thick with autumn. It is a little past midnight and I am sitting on a rock overlooking the non-existent harbour of Daniel's Harbour. The moon is yawning and stretching on the water, like it too will sleep. Like this town, like this entire world it seems. While I sit here, and marvel, at this beautiful beautiful land and how fundamentally, how utterly, unfamiliar it is to me. When I arrived it was novelty, and excitement, and it bore it's way into my head and heart and hands. It was present in my work, in my work day, that excitement, and it left me to sleep soundly. Now. Now. I enjoy it here, I truly do. But here there is nothing that catches my eye, my peripheral vision, and makes me forget where I am, forget my age. Nothing that makes me sink in comfort, in the secure and peaceful comfort of home. There is an absence here. A telling absence. I can feel it. As sure as I can feel the air leave my lungs, I can feel it. But, try as I might, I cannot, I cannot name it. I have a sad heart. I have a sad little, sore little heart. It would seem that there is a wound here that the nurse cannot mend.

ANGUS alone.

ANGUS
It was becoming regular. Our trips together. Me going with her up and down the coast. It was becoming regular and expected. Which was fine with me. Summer was giving it up, calling it quits. The woods were growing colourful and serious. As were

our talks. Fall was taking over. Days growing smaller. Seas
growing bigger.

MYRA and ANGUS in a boat.

MYRA
The day I left, the day the ship left port to cross the spring
Atlantic it was Friday the 13th of April. So, yes, I know of
superstition, know it's power. Grown men that day practically
weeping. Begging to set sail the day following. Tempting
providence they claimed, to set out on the 13th.

ANGUS
And you? What were you thinking? What were you feeling?

MYRA
Me? Many many things. But not fear.

ANGUS
Really.

MYRA
Really. Excitement more than anything else. Nothing could
happen to me to spoil the huge adventure upon which I was
embarking.

ANGUS smiles and begins to chuckle.

What? Why is that funny?

ANGUS
Just never heard anyone refer to Daniel's Harbour as an
adventure before.

MYRA
You just have to be on the outside looking in. You ever been
there?

ANGUS
On the outside? Yeah. Yeah I have.

MYRA
It's a confusing place.

ANGUS
Can be.

MYRA
This was, and continues to be a huge adventure. Believe you me.
As different from my world as night and day. My old world.

ANGUS
You getting anxious to get back?

MYRA
Doesn't matter. I'm contracted for another year and a half yet. And then, maybe longer. No roads in place.

ANGUS
What does that have to do with it?

MYRA
Give you two years of sensible help. Give you that and then leave here. Not even a road to get help down the coast, or up. You can't behave that way, think that way and call yourself a Christian.

ANGUS
No. I suppose not.

MYRA
No.

ANGUS
So you're here until they lay a road.

MYRA
See the adventure? You see it now? Gobbles you up. Two years turn to four turn to eight.

ANGUS
Or longer.

MYRA
Or longer. You just hope that, that that adventure is your fate. That grand story you're falling into is what is meant to be. How tragic otherwise. Fated to be elsewhere, providence tugging at your sleeve. And you not listening.

ANGUS
You believe in fate then. Providence.

She smiles at him.

I guess I do too. It gets jumbled up sometimes. Confusing. Needs to be sorted out. Needs you to take action. Decisions to be made.

MYRA
Is that so?

ANGUS

Yes. Very much so. I mean, my decision to move back here. To leave the merchant marines. To come back here. It's all fine and good to say that it was fate, but I could have just as easily walked away from it, been scared off by it. Stayed away. There are decisions involved, and, and I guess a person is never sure whether what they are doing is what is right, what is written. Who can say, whether I was supposed to come back here, and open a store. Get married. Have kids.

MYRA

Is that what you want? Do you know?

ANGUS

I think so. I don't know. Yes. Yes, that is what I want.

MYRA

Then. That is fate.

A small pause.

ANGUS

And what do you want?

MYRA

To help people.

ANGUS

For yourself. Do you know what you want for yourself?

She smiles and turns away from him.

MYRA

That, Mr. Bennett, is the problem entirely. Wouldn't you agree?

ANGUS alone.

ANGUS

I remember hearing those words. Her saying she was duty-bound. Here. For as long as it took to get a road. No two-year contract. No deadline. And sir, wasn't that a scary thing. Hearing that. Didn't that put things into another light. I there listening to that, and all I could sound was some talk of decisions, taking action. A collection of words falling out of my mouth like they were put there by someone else. I got to speak them. Then I got to pick them up, and bring them home to think about what they meant. Decision. Action.

MYRA and Helen.

WOMAN
She was only three you know. When Marie was born. That's
young. And while she said she always wanted a sister, well they
say that. They always do, until it's there, until there is another
face to look at, another attention-getter. So, we expected some
trouble. Had been warned about it in fact. Had been told that
she would act up. Heard every story under the sun. But when she
saw Marie. Oh my. Break your heart. The softest little voice. She
spoke with the softest little voice in telling us to shut it up, we'd
wake the baby. And she was like that. Always on about the baby.
Don't make a racket you'll wake the baby. Wanting to feed the
baby. Wanting to hold the baby. You wouldn't know but she was
a woman of forty the way she got on. You wouldn't know it at all.

Pause.

Yeah, she was a charmer.

MYRA
How is Marie?

WOMAN
Fine girl. Five months old last Tuesday. Soon off the milk, please
God. Big head a hair on her now too. Takes after her father for
sure.

MYRA
Is she well?

WOMAN
Oh yes girl. Finest kind.

MYRA
Dennis?

WOMAN
He's good. Working himself to death dragging in wood.
Convinced it's gonna be a bad one this year. No talking him
out of it.

MYRA
And you? How are you?

WOMAN
Good. I'm fine.

Pause.

Not much of a liar. I'm tired girl. Hard year.

MYRA
Hard week.

Helen stands and walks away from her.

WOMAN
More tea?

MYRA
No, no thank you. Helen.

WOMAN
You sure?

MYRA
Helen. Physically. How are you?

WOMAN
There's a lovely bit of bread there Nurse, some jam.

MYRA
Helen, please. Any pain? Discomfort? Coughing?

WOMAN
Nurse.

MYRA
It's important.

WOMAN
No. I'll not have you at that. It's too soon.

MYRA
Helen, there is a very real danger–

WOMAN
No. Sit here and let you frighten the wits out of me. No Nurse. It's too hard. Cassie only gone four days now. Four days and you talking the like of that.

MYRA
She died of a disease called TB, Helen, a very dangerous, very easy to catch disease–

WOMAN
Don't presume me ignorant Nurse. I know full well what she died of. I know full well too that we are fine. I know full well many a family that suffered through what we just did, suffered through it and lost but the one. The only thing this week, I swear to God the only thing this week that kept my body out of that hole with Cassie was the little one I had in my arms

and the man standing next to me. So don't you dare presume me ignorant, and don't you dare frighten me with the thought of that happening all over again.

MYRA
Helen–

WOMAN
Goodbye Nurse.

A small tense pause.

MYRA
I'm not trying to upset you. Helen, I'm not. I'll go, just.... Please just, humour me. Let me take a look at you. Listen to your lungs. Helen.

WOMAN
We're fine Nurse. We are. All of us. Now you're welcome to more tea, but I've got to get on the go. Dennis will be home the once. Marie needs to be fed.

Helen takes up Marie and rocks her. She sings softly.

MYRA
I thought myself fully prepared for any emergency, any medical emergency or situation that would, that could present itself here. And yet this place, these people, in all of their glory manage to surprise me. Not in the condition with which they present themselves, not with the illnesses. But with the stubbornness. The sheer stubbornness when it comes to taking care of themselves, with heeding my words. I had not foreseen having to lecture on the contagious nature of the tubercular patient.

Helen begins to breastfeed Marie.

It is like they think, or want to believe, that I am trying to scare them, assert some sort of authority which they assume I have given myself because of my title. Knowledge is, and has been my only authority. More than anything I want to share it. It is often exceedingly difficult to do so.

At the clinic.

ANGUS
Nurse?

MAN
Nurse?

WOMAN
Nurse?

MYRA
One at a time. One at a time. Yes?

WOMAN
Nurse, warts. Warts Nurse.

MYRA
What about them?

WOMAN
My grandmother said to rub a bit of meat on 'em and throw it to the dog. That work?

MYRA
Yes of course. If by meat you mean wood file, and by rub you mean saw off. Otherwise you can rub whatever you want for how ever long you want, but the only thing you'll be doing is feeding the dog. Next.

ANGUS
Nurse?

WOMAN
Nurse?

MAN
Nurse?

MYRA
Yes?

MAN
The wife gets the wicked nosebleeds. She swears to warding it off by tying a green ribbon about the neck.

MYRA
Absolutely.

MAN
Yeah?

MYRA
Just make sure you tie it tight enough.

ANGUS
Nurse?

MAN
Nurse?

WOMAN
Nurse?

MYRA
Yes, yes?

WOMAN
My youngest got the asthma. Now, they says that you should pluck a hair from the head, take her height on the wall, put the hair in a hole at just that spot, just at her head height, and plug it up, and once she grows past that hole, the hole with the hair in the wall what was her height, that she'll never have the asthma again. Now. What do you think of that?

MYRA
Madam, who told you this?

WOMAN
Young Charlie Payne, God rest his soul.

MYRA
Perhaps you should bring the child with you in the future. Next.

ANGUS
Nurse.

WOMAN
Nurse?

MAN
Nurse?

MYRA
Yes?

MAN
Father gave me a fishbone to carry in my pocket on account of my toothache.

MYRA
And does your father have any teeth left?

MAN
No.

MYRA
Lie down.

He lies on her table as she quickly produces her dental instruments.

MAN
Nurse!

ANGUS
Nurse?

WOMAN
Nurse?

MYRA
Yes. Yes. One at a time please.

MAN
Nurse!

WOMAN
Nurse?

ANGUS
Nurse?

MYRA
Yes. I'm busy.

WOMAN
Nurse?

ANGUS
Nurse!

She turns angrily from the young man's mouth.

MYRA
Yes?

ANGUS
Would you consider marrying me?

MYRA
Yes.

She turns back to the young man's mouth and gives a hard yank. The young man cries with pain. Lights out.

— • — Act Two — • —

ANGUS alone.

ANGUS
They will tell you now, they will tell you when you ask that she was hopelessly in love. Love at first sight is what they will tell you. They will tell you that that first time we met at Mom's house was the beginning of everything. An inevitable chain of events in which she was a helpless pawn to something bigger than herself. They will tell you that, and they are wrong.

MYRA and Mrs. House.

MYRA
Our marriage, our courtship is one of practicality. Plain and simple. Angus is without wife. I am without husband. I am in need of assistance in travel, the practicalities of getting to the patient.

ANGUS
I, apparently, was in need of a cook, a baker, a darner of socks, all of which she was becoming acquainted with by the way.

MYRA
It is a practical decision. Despite how it looks. And how he looks.

ANGUS
So, do not listen to them when they tell you that. When they speak of true love and fate and such nonsense.

MYRA
Angus Bennett is a very nice man whom it makes perfect sense to make my husband. Yes, that's what I'm talking about. It just makes sense.

ANGUS
And she'd say it to my face. Partly because she believed it. But partly because deep down she knew that I knew there was more there than that. Caution, excitement, determination. Pride. Like a shy child building a house of cards.

WOMAN
Well, it's wonderful. It is.

MYRA
It is that.

WOMAN
Yes. Certainly. Everyone thinks so.

MYRA
Yes.

WOMAN
Of course, all my crowd are climbing the walls over it. Ready to burst. Saying I told you so this, and I knew they'd get together that.

MYRA
It is a sound idea.

WOMAN
It's a wonderful thing.

MYRA
And a practical thing. Angus has been most helpful to me in the past months, getting back and forth. Assisting with patients.

WOMAN
Yes.

MYRA
And it would only make sense to make it official, our partnership as it were. And he needs a wife, a good wife.

WOMAN
He most certainly does.

MYRA
He needs that.

WOMAN
Nurse, are you all right?

A small pause.

MYRA
One could think it distasteful, this behaviour. To be anything but overjoyed, to be sitting here stewing in questions.

WOMAN
Jitters my child.

MYRA
Really. I mean, teeth, babies, this I can do. A household, cooking, baking.

WOMAN

Now your bread is fine. It is. It will be better, someday. With practice.

MYRA

With time. Which I may not have. Which I may never have. Running back and forth dealing with half of the coast. Is that fair? Honestly. Do you think that is fair?

WOMAN

Honestly?

MYRA

Honestly.

WOMAN

Honestly, I would have to say that Angus is many things, but slow he is not. Agreed.

MYRA

Certainly.

WOMAN

So then don't you think, don't you agree that in the last four months of helping you and your bags up and down this sorry coast it would have crossed his mind that this behaviour, this annoying behaviour of yours of wanting to help everyone and their sheep would be a behaviour that was not going to change quickly. Or at all. Don't you think he has the slightest idea of what he's getting himself into?

MYRA

I suppose so.

WOMAN

So what then, my dear, is the problem?

MYRA

I don't know. Perhaps, perhaps I don't know what I'm getting myself into.

WOMAN

Jitters.

MYRA

You think so?

WOMAN

Look Nurse, despite your claims that this marriage makes sense, that it is all about sense, I can assure you that it is bloody well not. Two people promising to stand by each other through anything, partners for life. Promises like that don't get made unless you're that drunk on each other that nothing else matters. Sense got nothing to do with it. If it was about sense, if you were all about sense, you probably wouldn't of even set foot in this place. Right? Right?

A small pause.

Nurse. Be happy. And be done with it.

MAN and WOMAN alone.

MAN
Oh, she was all nerves I hear.

WOMAN
Oh yes, I heard that.

MAN
What with her being from Britain and–

WOMAN
And Angus being from home.

MAN
Too different, see.

WOMAN
Afraid they'd be too different, culturally eh.

MAN
But sure she was one of us by that point.

WOMAN
Yes, practically one of us.

MAN
What with her keeping the chickens.

WOMAN
And the garden.

MAN
Making the boots and the floor mats.

WOMAN
And the jam, and the partridge, and the fish.

MAN
Shearing the sheep and weaving the wool.

WOMAN
She was never idle.

MAN
No sir. Not one second.

WOMAN
She wasn't cooking, she was cleaning.

MAN
She wasn't cleaning, she was birthing.

WOMAN
Or at the church, organizing the choir.

MAN
Playing the organ.

WOMAN
And then the medical stuff, what with the diarrhea.

MAN
And the flu.

WOMAN
And the pneumonia.

MAN
And the whooping cough.

MAN & WOMAN
Tuberculosis.

WOMAN
Bloody stuff.

MAN
Pulling out fish hooks.

WOMAN
Draining abscesses.

MAN
Stitching cuts.

WOMAN
Applying salves.

MAN
Sure it's a wonder the poor woman had the time to breathe let alone start a family.

WOMAN
That's for bloody well sure. It's a wonder they found time to
have Grace at all.

*MYRA enters on ANGUS at home. He sits wearily. A small pause
as she looks at him.*

MYRA
She down?

ANGUS
Finally. Didn't think she was going to sleep at all tonight.

MYRA
Misses her mother.

ANGUS
You look tired.

MYRA
No.

ANGUS
You've been on your feet all day.

MYRA
Nothing out of the ordinary.

ANGUS
You walk? Back from Portland Creek?

MYRA
Yes.

ANGUS
Sit.

MYRA
Angus.

ANGUS
No, sit. Let me get you some tea.

He leaves for tea. She is very much alone. A small pause.

MYRA
She must love you.

ANGUS
(off) What?

MYRA

She must love you. Spending all day with her. Spending most days with her.

ANGUS

(off) She's barely three months old. I don't think she even knows who I am yet.

She speaks quietly to herself. ANGUS re-enters and hears her.

MYRA

I think she does. I think she knows who you are.

A small pause.

ANGUS

Well, she will. Someday. She will know who I am. And you. And she'll boast about the two best parents on the coast. And her mother, the nurse.

MYRA smiles and turns away.

Work is work my dear. You do what you can. And the rest. The rest you ask for help.

MYRA

I can't take her with me.

ANGUS

And you can't not go. So. So we deal with it.

MYRA

It's that simple.

ANGUS

It's not simple. It just is. The fact of the matter is... Nurse, the fact of the matter is that child is never going to feel unloved, or unkept, or in need. Of anything. Is she.

MYRA

I love my husband very much.

ANGUS

Yeah?

MYRA

I love my husband very very much. Beyond words. Beyond report.

ANGUS

Better.

MYRA

I love my husband. And my baby. My beautiful little girl. And my beautiful little house.

ANGUS

Oh, now, don't start.

MYRA

It is Angus. It is a lovely little house you've built. I do love it.

ANGUS

Why?

MYRA

What?

ANGUS

Why do you love it? What about it do you love?

MYRA

That. That it's.

ANGUS

Yeah?

MYRA

Mine.

He smiles.

ANGUS

Ours.

MYRA

Ours. Ours.

A small soft kiss. A noise. He speaks softly to her.

ANGUS

Kettle's boiled.

He slowly rises to fetch it.

ANGUS alone.

It's foolishness to think that a wedding, a child will completely cure a person of homesickness. Of that loneliness. It's foolish to think that great happiness equals complete happiness. I never saw her as happy as she was the year Grace was born. I also never saw her as distant. She worked harder, to push it down, to keep it at bay. But you could see it in her eyes. As frustrating as it was you could see it in her eyes. Watching her out on the hill by herself. Wrapped in a blanket, watching the moon and the sea. And it was foolish to think it was just going to go away like that. As foolish as thinking that all it was was little case of homesickness.

MYRA alone on the hill.

MYRA

I have biked through bomb raids. I have watched people starve. I have watched children die. I have done all this with a pervasive sense of duty pushing me onwards. I have done all of this without succumbing to sentiment. I have never been soft, as a person that word has never defined me. I have also never stood over a patient and truly felt consequence, truly felt that my actions would have repercussions. They do certainly, always for the patient, their family. But I have never felt at risk, personally. As a person. That my soul lies in the balance, that it could very well split. I have never felt that. Not once. Not once. So what does that make me? Heartless? Cold? I feel love. Now more than ever. I do feel love and that helps dispel these concerns. Angus helps. Angus helps everything. Marrying him was the best thing I have ever done. I don't doubt that. But. But I feel very alone here. Yes, that is it. Sometimes I feel very alone, maybe, maybe just because of the sheer distance, separation from what I used to be, where I came from. Angus helps. Angus, and the work itself. The sheer frequency of it. And the variety.

MYRA enters on MAN.

MAN

This way Nurse. She's in here.

MYRA

How long has she been this way?

MAN

A day or so. Longer than a day. Too long.

MYRA

She's in pain?

MAN

Appears to be.

MYRA

I need you to relax. Everything is going to be okay.

MAN

Yes. Of course.

MYRA

Just tell me everything.

MAN

Well, I came in to check on her yesterday. Cause, cause she's been quiet lately. And I haven't been thinking anything of it. I mean she is quite old. It's natural she would have spurts like that. You know quiet spurts like that.

MYRA

Of course.

MAN

I didn't think anything of it.

MYRA

It's all right Fred.

MAN

And when I checked on her yesterday she was breathing strangely. Thick deep breaths. And stopping in between. Like she couldn't, couldn't catch her breath, or something. And her eyes were closing. Dropping. Like she was weak. Too weak to stand.

MYRA

She was lying down?

MAN

No, standing. But barely.

MYRA

She's been eating well?

MAN

Less than usual. Yes, that's for sure less than usual.

MYRA

Is she jumpy?

MAN

Regularly yes. Won't let no one near her but me. Now, who knows.

MYRA

I need to know. I need to know for my safety.

MAN

She, I guess she will be fine. I don't know.

MYRA
Anything else I should know?

MAN
Her stool is loose. Very loose, and, plentiful.

MYRA
Plentiful?

MAN
A bucket each time. Give or take. And.

MYRA
And?

MAN
Her mane is thinning. Thinning quite a bit.

MYRA
Alright. I'll do what I can.

She moves to go to the patient.

MAN
Nurse. Cleo is old. I know that. She's been good to us, and, and if this is all for her, I guess that's it and I should be grateful. But. But it's going to be awfully hard for us. This winter. Without her. It's gonna be hard getting the wood in. There's only me. Maud is no good for that stuff. It's gonna be awfully hard without her. Damn near impossible. I just.

MYRA
I'll do what I can Fred.

MAN
Yeah. I know. I know.

ANGUS alone.

ANGUS
What was she supposed to do? That's what she'd ask. Sit around and laze away the time. Turn people away at the door. Watch people around her lose their babies, their very lives. Because her contract ran out. She knew when she came here that she only had two years. But she said it herself. Leave people with no road, and no nurse. So, there you go. We got married, she settled down for the long haul knowing that officially, her time here would run out. And when it did her life was here. For better or worse, her life was here, and she was working. That's how it went. She went along as usual. Treating who needed to be treated. Helping who

needed to be helped. Take payment when she could. More often
not. Sometimes just taking what could be offered.

MYRA by a field.

WOMAN
Nurse.

MYRA
Mary, how are you?

WOMAN
Can't complain girl. Howard see you this morning?

MYRA
I've not been home Mary, I have to confess. Is his jaw bothering
him?

WOMAN
No, finally stopped his whining. Thanks to you. He was going to
drop over payment.

MYRA
Now Mary, I told Howard–

WOMAN
I'm full aware what you told Howard, and it's appreciated. But
fair is fair.

MYRA
If you insist. A sack of potatoes it is.

WOMAN
Potatoes?

MYRA
Yes, when Howard was over to finally have that tooth pulled he
offered me a sack of potatoes.

WOMAN
He did?

MYRA
Yes. Was he wrong to do so?

WOMAN
No. No girl it's not that it's...

MYRA
What?

WOMAN

Sure you got your own potatoes. Lovely field of 'em, I can see it from here.

MYRA

Yes.

WOMAN

More potatoes over there than your crowd would eat all winter.

MYRA

You obviously don't know my crowd.

WOMAN

Nurse.

MYRA

Yes?

WOMAN

Howard didn't offer you potatoes. He knows you don't need potatoes. I told him, I told him to pay you proper.

MYRA

And proper payment is a sack of potatoes.

WOMAN

Nurse.

MYRA

Mary I'm not going to barter with you I'm sorry, the tooth was pulled and you said so yourself, fair is fair.

WOMAN

Nurse. We can afford it. We can. We had a good year. Better than last. And, your generosity is noted, it's very kind. But, but we'd like to be square with you.

MYRA

Mary.

WOMAN

I'm serious Nurse. We want to be square.

MYRA

And I want you to be. I've more use for your fine potatoes than I do for that bit of money. What am I going to spend it on? Something at my own husband's shop?

WOMAN

Nurse–

MYRA

Ah Mary, just give me the potatoes. You don't want to see me angry.

WOMAN

You are as stubborn as they say.

MYRA

Not stubborn Mary. Just a lover of a fine potato. How are you otherwise?

WOMAN

Good girl. Not long for this stuff now.

MYRA

No I wouldn't say. What are you, eight months?

WOMAN

Eight and a half.

MYRA

Shouldn't be at it at all really.

WOMAN

Got to get done girl. It all got to get done.

MYRA

I suppose so.

WOMAN

How is little Grace?

MYRA

Growing like a weed. They do that you know.

WOMAN

Can't wait.

MYRA

Take care of yourself Mary.

> *MYRA goes to leave.*

WOMAN

Yes girl. Going to have to call it quits the once. Can barely bend over anymore.

> *A pause as MYRA turns back to watch her work.*

No easy work on this coast.

MYRA
She is a fine person. Her husband as well. Generous with what they have. Their first child is due, and it is no secret to anyone who knows them that their glory days are ahead. Wanted children since they were children. It's a nice excitement that way. When people are excited to the point that others are excited for them. It's nice. Because they have worked hard for it. For everything. She continues to work hard. Tending a garden in her ninth month. Bending and tending with a belly full with child. A belly full with child with only so much room to move.

MYRA walks back to her.

Mary. Stoop. Like this. Don't bend.

WOMAN
What?

MYRA
Humour me. Don't bend at your hips like that. Stoop, with your legs, lift with your legs like this.

WOMAN
Why?

MYRA
It might help. Be easier. For everyone.

WOMAN
What?

MYRA
Humour me.

WOMAN
Like this?

MYRA
Yes.

WOMAN
Stooping.

MYRA
Instead of bending.

ANGUS enters.

ANGUS
Breach births at a frequency seemingly unheard of. Especially in the late summer, early fall. So many other problems here with

nutrition and sickness, I suppose for the longest while she just assumed it was part and parcel of the bigger picture. And then one day she gets it. Fall, and the harvest, and the bending and the babies.

MYRA

Mothers themselves unwarily forcing their little ones to turn in the womb. Forcing them out feet first.

ANGUS

It was such common sense you think some of our crowd would have come up with it. But no sir. Sharp as a tack she was. For picking up on that. Everyone thought so. Sure they published her ideas on that stuff in some fancy medical journal. Which is good. Very good. Only thing better is the number of normal births that wouldn't have been otherwise. Number of mothers with a bearable amount of pain in labour. Number of babies to live to thank her one day.

MYRA alone on a path. A pause.

MYRA

It is not my surroundings. Cause is virtually non-existent. But the feeling is there. I am standing in the middle of the path and it feels like, it feels like something is going horribly wrong. Or has already. That loneliness. It happens when I'm travelling alone like this. When my mind has reign to drift. I am standing in the middle of the path and there is not a breath of wind or sound of any kind. And there is nobody near. And I feel this well of doubt. A sense of absence. That none of this was meant to be. And in the midst of that, in the middle of that horrible sensation, my mind is as calm as the wind. My emotions as still as the grass.

A small pause.

It. It is troubling, that.

ANGUS enters.

ANGUS

You could see it on her face. Plain as day. And you were helpless to change it. Because it was never about you. It wasn't about anything you could touch or talk about. But it was real, and it was there. And you could see it on her face. Until that night.

MYRA and ANGUS in bed. A long silent pause. MYRA awakens.

MYRA
I have learned to sleep with my ears active. Alive to the night.

A pause as her eyes dart around the room.

They learned to filter. They learned to separate the common from the extraordinary. The wind rocking the windows from the knock on the door. The sea on the beach from the clatter of approaching hooves. The rattle of Angus' sleeping breath, from sleigh bells beating a path through the woods. Angus, wake up.

ANGUS
What?

MYRA
Listen.

MAN comes bursting in.

MAN
Nurse! Nurse Bennett!

MYRA
What's happened?

MAN
Accident ma'am.

MYRA
Where?

MAN
Horrible accident ma'am.

MYRA
Where?

MAN
Logging camp. Logging camp ma'am. Angus.

ANGUS
No.

MAN
It's Alex.

ANGUS
No.

MYRA
And that's that. We run. We get ourselves, as though by instinct, not even thinking, we get ourselves into the sleigh and we ride.

We are hours out. And yet the urgency, the sheer need of us getting there as quickly as possible has us in a sweat. Angus is like I've never seen him. That worry. In his eyes. In his body, everywhere. I can even see it in myself. We are all grabbing onto something. The sleigh, the reins, my medical bag, clutching tightly as though we ourselves, our exertion could affect the speed of the horse that leads us. And as we ride we listen. To the story. To what awaits us.

MAN

He was safe Nurse. He was always safe. But it was icy. Ice everywhere. And he slipped. His foot, he went under the saw. But he was fine. He was safe. He landed, his foot landed safely in the dust pit below the blade. But, his reflexes, he couldn't help but jump, pull back. And the blade caught him. Across the ankle. I believe it's gone. I believe his foot is gone clear off.

ANGUS

And all I could think about was Alex the silly fool dancing with the Nurse at that party. Throwing her around the kitchen like there was no tomorrow. I don't think I was worried. I don't think I ever really worried when she was near.

MYRA

And we are there. In the middle of the woods. The middle of the night. And there are men everywhere. And everyone is strangely quiet. Just looking at me as if to say, get on with it. And the lanterns are hitting the snow and lighting up the place, bouncing off the trees. And all I can see is this huge black spot in the middle of it all. Everyone is looking at this huge black spot in this sea of white. And I realize it is Alex. And then I realize it is Alex's blood. Hello Alex.

MAN

Nurse.

MYRA

And the light is closer now and you can see the colour of it. All red, and white of snow. Strangely like Christmas, and the thought of it makes me so sad and sick. And lying in the middle of it all is sweet sweet Alex. So in shock by that point he didn't even know what was what.

MAN

I told them they shouldn't bother you.

MYRA

No?

MAN

No. This time of night. Don't even hurt anymore.

MYRA

Alex, your foot.

MAN

Yes girl. Something ain't it. Weird looking.

MYRA

We have to get you up. And on the sleigh.

MAN

I can't walk, I don't think.

MYRA

That's alright.

MAN

Don't even hurt anymore though. Shouldn't have bothered you. Could have all waited until morning.

MYRA

It is no different. Fundamentally. It is no different. A patient is a patient. You function as you were taught. Your mind races for a practical solution even though one is probably not to be found. You file through procedures, interventions in your mind. Pages of text books, voices of mentors and teachers, doctors, in your ears. Stop the bleeding. Save the foot if you can, but stop the bleeding. This is all I think about on the way back to the house. My husband is beside me. His brother's blood on his shirt and I am too busy. My mind is too busy to offer consolation.

ANGUS

We arrived back at the house and she was barking commands.

MYRA

Angus. Go wake Mrs. House, and Mrs. Buckle. I need them immediately.

ANGUS

Yes Nurse.

MYRA

Mrs. House. Take this lint. I need you to sew bags, bags about this size. Quickly you need not be tidy.

WOMAN

Yes Nurse.

MYRA

Angus. Get your shovel. Fill the bags as they are ready. Fill them with snow.

ANGUS

Yes Nurse.

MYRA

Mrs. House. Pack the bags around Alex's leg. Here and here. As many as you can. They start to melt and you replace them. You understand?

WOMAN

Yes Nurse.

MYRA

Angus. Boil the kettle. Sterilize some water and these instruments. Quickly.

ANGUS

Yes Nurse.

MYRA

Alex. I'm going to clean your leg. You may feel discomfort.

MAN

Yes Nurse.

MYRA

I'm going to sew your foot back on Alex. I'm going to sew your foot back on. These bags, these bags of ice will help with the pain. They will help but not entirely. You must trust me Alex. You must remain calm and trust me. Trust me. Trust me.

ANGUS, WOMAN & MAN

Yes Nurse.

ANGUS

And that's what she did. She sewed, she stitched his foot back on. Cleaned it as best she could. Fragments of bone and old blood. Deadened his leg with lint bags filled with snow. And did her best. Did all she could do.

MYRA

He needs a doctor. A proper doctor to look at it. He's not going to bleed to death. I've seen to that. But I am no surgeon. And what I did tonight.... Angus, I have no aspirations of saving his foot. My instincts tell me, that he will lose it. But he must see a doctor. An injury like that, infection is all too possible. He. He is not safe yet. He needs to see a doctor.

MYRA, ANGUS, and WOMAN at telegraph office.

ANGUS
It was that next day she sent the telegram to the doctor in Bonne Bay.

MYRA
Young man with severed right foot. In need of your attention immediately. Request you come as soon as possible. Instructions for interim care vital.

ANGUS
It was the day after that when she got her reply.

WOMAN reads to her.

WOMAN
Can do more for him here. Sounds like an amputation case.

MYRA
Well?

ANGUS
Well.

MYRA
60 miles Angus.

ANGUS
At least.

MYRA
Do you think we can make it?

ANGUS
I don't know.

MYRA
I checked him this morning. Took off his bandages to see if.... He's looking better. His foot is taking some blood. At least. He might be able to make it through. Make that 60 miles.

ANGUS
Yeah.

MYRA
And he might not be able to make it otherwise.

ANGUS
Good then. We go.

MYRA
You think.

ANGUS
I'll get us there.

MYRA
I know you'll try.

ANGUS
I'll get us there. Okay?

MYRA
Yes.

     He walks away from her.

Angus?

ANGUS
Yeah.

     A small pause.

MYRA
Nothing.

     MYRA and ANGUS travelling.

We have done this before. That is what I keep telling myself.
We have made this trip before. Maybe not this early in the year.
Maybe not with this kind of cold. This much snow. Maybe not
this distance, in such a very real hurry. Maybe not with my
brother-in-law silent on a sleigh. Maybe not with all of that. But
we have made this trip before. That is what I keep telling myself.
Angus. Angus the snow is too deep. Too soft. She going in with
every step. Angus she is going in with every step.

ANGUS
Maybe by the coast.

MYRA
The drift ice.

ANGUS
Maybe clearer.

MYRA
Maybe? Angus.

ANGUS
I know.

MYRA
Slippery Angus. At all angles.

ANGUS
I know.

MYRA
It will be hard.

ANGUS
It'll be alright.

MYRA
And that's what we do. I am walking. There is no time to stop.
There is no time to pause and properly survey my surroundings.
I am walking and my head is turning and eyes are scanning and
I see nothing. Oh God I see nothing. Countless times I have
made this trip, or other's like it. We have done this before. But
never, never when I have travelled with Angus have I seen the
emptiness. The vastness of what we are trying to conquer. Never
has a distance seemed so great or impassable. Never have I felt
secretly, so secretly that I will not make it. That this vastness
will be the end of me. Of us. Of Alex. I am watching Angus
and his bravery, and Alex and his pain, and I am feeling so
thoroughly... afraid. I will admit it. Terrified of where I am.
Where I have gotten myself. I love Angus, I do not doubt that,
but I am having fear attack me on all sides. My God there is
nothing out here, and this man, this man, my brother, Alex, his
foot, his life rest with me. And I have known that responsibility,
I have held that power in my hands, fought it, conquered it, lost
to it. But now, here, I don't want to live if I lose. I cannot live to
see Alex die, to see Angus see Alex die. I am afraid like never
before, because I've never had so much to lose. I've never had
so much to lose. I will not lose this Angus! I will not lose this!
Angus!

ANGUS
Nurse. Look.

A long long motionless pause.

MYRA
And. There they are.

ANGUS
Help.

MYRA
Eight beautiful souls trekking toward us over the ice.

ANGUS
Parsons Pond. Must have intercepted our wire.

MYRA
Intercepted our wire and immediately mobilized to help.

ANGUS
I was getting afraid for a minute we wouldn't make it. The mare.

MYRA
I have had doubts, since I've been here, creeping in and begging
an audience. I have seen myself in England, in a quaint country
hospital. I have seen safety and convention and sanity and God
help me I have wanted it. My feet have been cold, tired, my legs
dying. I have lost patients to the stupidest of reasons. And
amidst it all I have seen a life that could well have been and it
looked so good. And put me out here, strip it all away until there
is nothing left here but something to lose, and the means to lose
it. And let me see it, see this. Eight men coming toward us.
Shaking our hands. Unhitching our mare. Lifting Alex. Eight
men with their strength and generosity as much a part of this
place as the snow and the wind. Let me see that, and every
doubt is all gone. And I am completely here, and ready, and able.
And I can stare down the devil himself.

MYRA near a stove.

WOMAN
How are ya maid?

MYRA
Cold.

WOMAN
No doubt. Here.

MYRA
Thank you.

WOMAN
Heard the wire, no way we couldn't help. In some way.

MYRA
Alex.

WOMAN
He's resting fine. Get yourself warmed up before you worries about him.

MYRA
How much further?

WOMAN
Eh?

MYRA
To Bonne Bay.

WOMAN
Forty. Forty-five mile.

A small pause.

MYRA
Alright.

ANGUS alone.

ANGUS
And that was the way it was. We went like that. From Parson's Pond. To Sally's Cove. From Sally's Cove to Bonne Bay. 60 miles in all.

MYRA
Long way to have come.

ANGUS
People offered assistance at every step. Food, shelter. Word made its way down the coast ahead of us. Always ahead of us. And it was like, as fast as we were moving, something was moving faster. Jumping the rocks and the tuckamore, the ice and snow. Burning a trail of hope and good humour. Something as light and real as the air filling your lungs. Don't know what you'd call it.

MYRA and WOMAN alone.

WOMAN
Here. Drink this.

MYRA
You are an angel.

WOMAN
Well that's high praise. Coming from you. Miracle worker.

MYRA
I don't know about that.

WOMAN
That's really something. What you did. 60 miles. 60 miles in that. Walking. And his foot. You, you sewed it on eh? Just sewed it on.

MYRA
Yes.

WOMAN
With a needle and thread like that. That's all.

MYRA
That's all.

WOMAN
You got some stomach on ya girl. I wouldn't want to be at that.

MYRA
One does what one has to do.

WOMAN
You warm enough?

MYRA
I'm fine, thank you.

WOMAN
Doctor will have me killed if I don't afford you every comfort.

MYRA
I couldn't be better.

A small pause.

WOMAN
Can I ask you a question?

MYRA
By all means.

WOMAN
It's a personal one, is all. Don't mean to pry.

MYRA
It's all right. Ask.

WOMAN
Do you know you're pregnant?

A small pause.

MYRA
Yes.

WOMAN
Well. Ain't that something.

MYRA
Three months.

WOMAN
Ain't that something. 60 miles.

A small pause. All smiles.

Well. Congratulations.

MYRA
Thank you.

ANGUS and MYRA.

ANGUS
To hear people talk of it now. The big deal they will make. The big story they will make of it. Talk about the cold and the ice like they were there themselves, the blood on the snow. Tell you how the doctor didn't need to amputate after all. That she had done a good enough job of it stitching it on that circulation resumed. Talk about how she saved Alex's foot. Against all odds.

MYRA
They'll tell you all that.

ANGUS
She would say.

MYRA
But they won't tell you that he still walks with a limp.

ANGUS smiles.

ANGUS
It was what it was. And she never had time for praise. A patient in need of a doctor. So you bring him. That's it.

MYRA
People get foolish about that kind of thing. Tell stories. Draw attention to it.

ANGUS
No big story to hear her tell it. That night. That long cold trip down the coast. That fact that she was pregnant with Trevor. None of it. Just happened. Like anything else. Like everything up to that point. Young Nurse moves to the edge of the world for two years. Marries humble, and devilishly handsome, local. Has family. Pulls teeth. Delivers babies. Saves lives.

He looks at her.

And stays.

MYRA
Being useful. Sure, that's why any one of us is put here. To make use of the time we're given. A person couldn't expect praise for it.

MAN and WOMAN alone.

MAN
Nurse Myra Bennett.

WOMAN
Honorary Member, Association Of Registered Nurses of Newfoundland.

MAN
Doctor of Science, *Honoris Causa*, Memorial University of Newfoundland.

WOMAN
Medal of the British Empire.

MAN
King George V Jubilee Award.

WOMAN
The Order of Canada.

MAN
King George VI Coronation Medal.

WOMAN
Queen Elizabeth II Coronation Medal.

MAN
Extractor of over 5000 teeth.

WOMAN
Midwife to over 700 births.

MAN
Mother of three.

WOMAN
Foster mother of four.

MAN
Died April 26, 1990.

WOMAN smiles.

WOMAN
Age one hundred years.

MAN
Her secret for a long life?

WOMAN
Hard work, a sense of humour particularly, more or less contented mind, ordinary food, no booze, no cigarettes. That's all.

MYRA looking out. ANGUS walks up behind her.

ANGUS
You hungry?

MYRA
No, but you must be.

ANGUS
I can wait.

MYRA
A few more minutes.

ANGUS
They will be here for a few days yet.

MYRA
Yes. Slow work.

ANGUS
It can be.

MYRA
A great deal of bog to contend with.

ANGUS
And rock.

MYRA
And rock.

ANGUS
They'll rip out a path, fill it, then lay down gravel for the road.

She smiles.

Good bit of work to be done. And plenty of time to see it. Come in. They will still be here tomorrow.

MYRA
I know.

ANGUS
And so will you.

MYRA
Yes.

They slowly begin to walk off stage.

I darned your lovely socks Mrs. House made for you. They have toes again.

ANGUS
You're a good hand girl, you're a good hand.

They leave the stage.

The end.

photo by Andrea Hann

Robert Chafe is a playwright and actor born and currently residing in St. John's, Newfoundland. He is an award-winning author of twelve plays, and co-author of another ten, all of which have seen production in Newfoundland and other parts of Canada. He is best known for his collaborations with director/designer Jillian Keiley (*Under Wraps, Emptygirl, Signals*) and director Danielle Irvine (*Place of First Light, Charismatic Death Scenes, Lemons*). He is currently Playwright in Residence for Artistic Fraud of Newfoundland.